RIDE WITH ME

Ride With Me

A Journey In His Presence

Kathy Gidley

XULON PRESS

Xulon Press
555 Winderley Pl, Suite 225
Maitland, FL 32751
407.339.4217
www.xulonpress.com

© 2023 by Kathy Gidley

All rights reserved solely by the author. The author guarantees all contents are original and do not infringe upon the legal rights of any other person or work. No part of this book may be reproduced in any form without the permission of the author.

Due to the changing nature of the Internet, if there are any web addresses, links, or URLs included in this manuscript, these may have been altered and may no longer be accessible. The views and opinions shared in this book belong solely to the author and do not necessarily reflect those of the publisher. The publisher therefore disclaims responsibility for the views or opinions expressed within the work.

Unless otherwise indicated, Scripture quotations taken from the King James Version (KJV) – *public domain*.

Unless otherwise indicated, Scripture quotations taken from the New King James Version (NKJV). Copyright © 1982 by Thomas Nelson, Inc. Used by permission. All rights reserved.

Paperback ISBN-13: 978-1-66288-962-2
Ebook ISBN-13: 978-1-66288-963-9

Dedication

TO MY FAITHFUL and loving husband, Mark, who is so supportive in my times of needing a quiet place. My dear husband, you guard like no other. I am so thankful that you love our dear Savior, and you are in pursuit of Him fervently. To be able to run together after the heart of the Lord with you is such an incredible journey.

To my sweet loving family, I am so thankful and proud that you are servants in the Kingdom of our Lord. You love Jesus and are encouragers and have been wonderful proofreaders. You are solid gold.

Special Thanks

I MUST SAY a huge "thank you" to Dr Dale Fife who has led the way to the Secret Place. Dr Fife is the author of "The Secret Place", "The Hidden Kingdom", "Spirit Wind" and many others that give us the understanding of the place of HIS presence. Thank you, Dr Fife, for your obedience and sharing from your experience. You are a treasure to the Kingdom of our dear Savior. It is by feasting on the revelations you offered to the body of Christ that I have found this precious place. Your gift of friendship to Mark and myself is more valuable than we can ever be able to express. Thank you to my sweet friend, Ginger Reed, for poring through my writing and helping me. You are a gift from the Lord.

Finally, Michele Gunn (Firebrand Studios), thank you for helping me give birth to this baby, my first book. You are such a tremendous blessing!

Thank you to my family and friends for reading and proofreading. I couldn't have done this without all of you.

Endorsements

I have known Kathy Gidley for over 20 years.

After reading her journal of the experience she had with the Lord, I had a hunger birthed in me to get to know Him in a greater way.

As you read this account you will laugh, you will cry, but most of all, you too, will have a desire to meet this Jesus that Kathy met.

You will NEVER be the same.

Lois Hoshor, Evangelist/Author

"What Kathy Gidley has presented in *'Ride With Me'* is not just another recitation of one person's unique experiences, but a profoundly simple invitation for every reader to share personal intimacy with Jesus. She manages to convey her awe at the atmosphere of Heaven while teaching rich truths of walking out the most authentic Christian life. Every new believer, struggling follower, and seasoned saint needs a copy of *'Ride With Me'* right beside their Bible. I have been refreshed and delighted delving into these glorious experiences alongside her and inspired to spend more time with my Savior."

Michele Gunn, Firebrand Studios

Kathy has such a gift to see and sense the things of the Spirit realm and to engage in the presence of the Lord in such a transparent way. This book will propel you into a deeper relationship and greater encounters with the Lord, as you can't help but hunger for more of Him when you get wrapped up in these divine testimonies of God's leading which are the fruit of Kathy's authentic journey and lifestyle of intimacy with God.

Kent Mattox, Founder of Word Alive International Outreach

Do you desire your heart to be stirred? Do you wish for an intimacy with the Father that is greater than anything you have ever encountered before? Kathy Gidley found this and you can discover it as well. Take a journey with Kathy as she shares her own encounters with the Father. She found a way to quiet herself before the Lord and then simply ask Him, "Lord, I am going to take this quiet time and wait before You. Do You have anything on Your heart that You would like to talk to me about? I'm going to quiet myself and listen." What Kathy discovered is Father has much He wants to talk with us about.

As I read this book, there were many times I felt I was intruding on such a sacred moment between Father and daughter – as though I was overhearing something I shouldn't and should walk away. But then Father God would scoop me up and compel me to join them. And I would. You can too. You can have your own journey and intimacy with the Lord. Father God has a Secret Place where He is waiting to meet with you.

This is a must read for everyone. This is one of those books that will so impact your life making you yearn for a deeper journey with Father God. I highly recommend this book and I highly recommend Kathy Gidley. Pick it up and take it home with you today.

Mark Hawkins, Founder / Pray Alabama

FOREWORD

Exploring the Heavens

THE MORNING SUN shimmered on the gentle waves of Tampa Bay, reflecting off the luxurious turquoise surface provoking visions and dreams of paradise. I was captured by its alluring beauty and transported in my imagination to a tropical island in the Caribbean Sea. Palm trees embraced the soft southern trade winds like a mother caressing her child. I lounged on a swaying hammock beneath the palms, a cold Coke in my hand and kettle drum music playing nearby. My reverie was abruptly shattered by a commanding voice.

"Cut the engine!" Captain Charlie ordered. "I want to teach you a vitally important principle of navigation."

The rude awakening shocked me back to reality. *I am here to learn how to become a ship's captain. This is not a pleasure cruise!* I reminded myself. I pulled the throttle to idle and shut the engine off. The sudden silence forced me to focus on our location. We were floating about ten yards from the Number Two red navigation buoy in the silken silence of gentle undulating waves on the Intracoastal Waterway. *"What could Charlie possibly have to teach me from this vantage point in the middle of Tampa Bay?"* I speculated.

She pointed to a barely visible object on the distant shoreline far to the south on Anna Maria Island. "Dale, do you see that tall tree jutting up on the island? Fix your eyes on that navigation point. That is your destination!" She announced. "But you have a very serious problem; **you can't get there from here!**"

"What do you mean? Why, that's ridiculous! Of course, I can get there from here." I replied, challenging her certitude.

She explained, "If you set a straight course for that location, you will go aground on dangerous sand bars lurking just below the surface. The only way to get there safely is to follow your chart and pay close attention to your depth finder. You must zig-zag your way to the distant shore. *The best and safest course is not always the shortest one.*"

What I learned as a novice that day under the tutelage of an experienced captain with trans-oceanic experience changed my understanding of navigation not only on the rivers, lakes, and oceans of the world, but in my personal life. This truth has become a principle which has brought understanding to my spiritual journey. Many times, what I thought was a detour was really the waypoint for a vital lesson I needed to learn. Only by hindsight did I see the guiding hand of God directing me along the way. *We live life forward but understand it backward.*

Whatever goal you have set in your life, I can guarantee that you won't get there in a straight line. When you finally arrive at your destination, you will look back at the course you have taken with amazement. You will realize that God had a purpose for each deviation you had to take. Each zig or zag is a new lesson to be learned.

This is why I want to highly recommend Kathy Gidley's book, *Ride with Me*. I have known Kathy and her husband, Dr. Mark Gidley, for over fifteen years. They pastor a spiritually alive and thriving church in Gadsden, Alabama. She is a worship leader, intercessor, and teacher, an amazing mother and grandmother giving wise counsel and love to her family, and

Exploring the Heavens

her vivacious, fun-loving spirit always brings joy to others. Her exemplary life and spiritual passion emanate through every word of *Ride with Me*.

After many years of serving God, Kathy discovered that the traditional practices of spiritual discipline were insufficient to quench the passion in her heart for God's intimate presence. She realized that ***she couldn't get there from here***. So, her journey into the presence of God took on a new direction that led her to unexpected and unplanned places in the spirit. Now, intimacy with God is a daily adventure for her. Kathy's book, *Ride with Me* will awaken you to a whole new way of engaging God's presence. This is exactly what God desires for all of us. Please don't read *Ride with Me* like it's just another book. It is so much more. It is the Captain's log of a seasoned pneumanaut (Spirit led explorer), written to encourage, inform, and instruct you on **HOW TO GET THERE FROM HERE**.

If you want to motivate people to build a boat, giving them the tools and materials to build it will not suffice. You must start by telling them where the boat can take them. *Ride with Me* does exactly that! You will discover the mystery of visions in the heavenly realms. You may even receive healing in your own life as you witness the mercy and immensity of love exuding from God. Secret doorways, portals and pathways that lead to intimacy with God, previously unknown to you, will suddenly appear and beckon you to enter. Your Bible will come alive with revelation knowledge that was previously invisible to you. But this life-changing adventure in the spirit requires you to take the first step. As Kathy puts it, "Will you accept the invitation to *ride with Him?*"

This is a new season on God's calendar. It's time for you to leave the old ways and join the thousands of Christians who have embraced all that Jesus has prepared for you. Be bold and courageous. Break out of the old wineskin of tradition and the religious straitjacket that forces you to conform to the dictates of men. I encourage you to pray the following prayer written by Saint Brendan who was also known as The Navigator. Allegedly, he set sail in a small coracle of wood and ox hide from Ireland and ended up in Newfoundland, an amazing achievement back in the 5th century. His life and legacy are a gift to all of us who dare to boldly step into the unfamiliar with Jesus.

The Prayer of St. Brendan

Help me to journey beyond the familiar
and into the unknown.
Give me the faith to leave old ways
and break fresh ground with You.
Christ of the mysteries, I trust You
to be stronger than each storm within me.
I will trust in the darkness and know
that my times, even now, are in Your hand.
Tune my spirit to the music of heaven,
and somehow, make my obedience count for You.

It's time to tune your spirit to the music of heaven! *Ride with Me* is a wonderful starting point. Enjoy the journey. You WILL get there from here but expect the unexpected!

Dr Dale A Fife
Founder and President of Mountain Top Global Ministries
Author of The Secret Place, Passionately Pursuing
God's Presence

Preface

I WOULD NEVER have thought that a time of "shut down" could bring such a tremendous experience into my life. My husband Mark had left me alone for a few days to visit his brother; right on the heels of his return, we were quarantined. In that time alone, I began a journey with God that can only be described as amazing. I had my daily Bible study, prayer and worship, and then I thought, "Lord, I am going to take this quiet time and wait before You. Do You have anything on Your heart that You would like to talk to me about? I'm going to quiet myself and listen."

Incredibly, He began to stir my heart. In a series of visions, He made Himself known to me in ways that cause me to stand in awe and sheer adoration of Him. He is pure love, and there is none like Him in all the earth.

When I speak of having visions, I am awake, not in a trance. As I focus on Him, I see pictures or short movies playing in my imagination. In this instance, they were more intense than those I had experienced in the past, and I found myself amazed at the revelation from Holy Spirit which opened my understanding of spiritual truths.

I am very intent about guarding myself in these times with the Lord, weighing each experience with the Word of God. He has taught me how to recognize my own emotions and cast them aside to keep my heart pure. On this journey with Lord, I am determined that my flesh will not get in the way of His message to me. I've chosen to share even the times that Jesus had correction for me, in the hope that you will learn from my growing pains. I continue to learn as I seek Him.

I believe every child of God has the invitation to be in His presence. He wants to engage us in our prayer time. All we must do is make ourselves available by coming before Him, quieting our hearts and minds, and waiting for Him to speak to us. His amazing invitation is found in His word: *"Behold, I stand at the door and knock. If anyone hears My voice and opens the door, I will come in to him and dine with him, and he with me." (Revelation 3:20 NKJV)* If we invite Him, He will come in and feed us with His presence.

The journey of personal encounters with God begins when we pause and wait. It seems backwards to us, because in our natural world our days begin with waking and activity. But in the spirit realm with God, we must be still and listen. Be quiet. Settle our hearts and minds. Only then can we "hear" what God is saying to us in that still small voice. In my encounters, He speaks in pictures and visions; your journey may take a different form. Our Lord has much to share with us.

This book is my way to share my experiences with God in the "secret place", the precious time when I truly get quiet before Him and learn from Him. I hope it will encourage you to hunger for His presence and seek Him out. My friends, it is worth every moment! I invite you to join me in an adventure of your own.

Lamentations 3:25-26
NKJV

*25 The Lord is good to those who **wait** for Him,
To the soul who seeks Him.*

*26 It is good that one should hope and **wait quietly**
for the salvation of the Lord.*

~ Table of Contents ~

Introduction xxv

Introduction of Abraham and Opening Spiritual Eyes

Journal Entry Day 1:   The Invitation & Meeting Abraham 5
Journal Entry Day 2:   Opening My Spiritual Eyes 11

Healing for the Journey

Journal Entry Day 3:   Inner Healing for the Journey Ahead ... 20
Journal Entry Day 4:   Deeper Healing of the Past 30

Learning to Move in the Heavenlies – Veils, Gates, Portals, Doorways

Journal Entry Day 5:   Learning to Move in the Heavenlies – the Veils 38
Journal Entry Day 6:   The Heavenlies Contain His Story 43
Journal Entry Day 7:   He is Far Beyond The Heavenlies 50

The Significance of Worship

Journal Entry Day 8:   Worship and Revival 58
Journal Entry Day 9:   Worship in Pureness 63

Moving Into Other Dimensions

Journal Entry Day 10:   Prayer Time & Another Dimension 71
Journal Entry Day 11:   The Lamb's Book of Life 78

Traveling Instructions

Journal Entry Day 12: Keep Your Load Light...................85
Journal Entry Day 13: Viewpoint of Heaven 91
Journal Entry Day 14: By Him, For Him, From Him 94

Assignments

Journal Entry Day 15: Assignments – Thy Kingdom Come....99
Journal Entry Day 16: Assignment to Intercession..........103
Journal Entry Day 17: His Voice 109
Journal Entry Day 18: Intercession Over Cities.............112
Journal Entry Day 19: His Wonderful Creatures............117
Journal Entry Day 20: Renewing My Mind 121
Journal Entry Day 21: The Calling of Intercession 126
Journal Entry Day 22: Intercession Assignment: Jerusalem...130
Journal Entry Day 23: The Watchtower – Insights for Watchmen........................134
Journal Entry Day 24: Assignment for the Harvest..........137

Kingdom Placement, Kingdom Equipping & Kingdom Protocol

Journal Entry Day 25: Kingdom Placement and Equipping ... 143
Journal Entry Day 26: Kingdom Equipping.................148
Journal Entry Day 27: Equipping and Gifting 153
Journal Entry Day 28: Feeding the Multitude 157
Journal Entry Day 29: Go to the Thirsty...................162
Journal Entry Day 30: God's Amazing Love.................166
Journal Entry Day 31: Raining Oil........................170
Journal Entry Day 32: Equipped and Released 174
Journal Entry Day 33: This Isn't Abraham..................178
Journal Entry Day 34: Signs and Wonders..................179
Journal Entry Day 35: Kingdom Protocol...................185
Journal Entry Day 36: Gentle Reminder of Protocol.........192
Journal Entry Day 37: Father's Kitchen: Provision..........195
Journal Entry Day 38: God's Provision of Wisdom & Revelation 201

Journal Entry Day 39:   Praying in the Courtroom of Heaven... 204

The Warning

Journal Entry Day 40:   Warning of What is Coming 209

Summary 213
Appendix 215
Endnotes 221

Introduction

THIS PUBLICATION MOST definitely is not meant to be "scripture", nor is it ever to replace scripture. There is only one Bible, one Word of God. Every experience we have in our personal experiences with Him must line up with His Holy Word, because God does not contradict Himself.

Each of my journal entries is the story of one of my encounters with the Lord. In the first experience, the Lord extends an invitation to me to 'ride' with Him. In my opinion, there is no answer but a resounding, "YES, LORD!" By accepting His request, I learn the mystery of visions in the heavenly realm. Next, I submit to a time of healing in His presence; a must for me before I can go any further. He then begins to lead me in traveling through the heavenlies in varying ways by seeing doors, portals, gateways, veils. As I move with Him in these beautiful visions, I receive a deeper understanding of spiritual truths from the Bible. That focus pulls me into a greater desire to bring others into this great Kingdom of our Lord, a need to intercede for our nation and community, and a time of equipping me for my purpose in the Kingdom. The greatest lesson I brought away from this experience is God's immense love for us. It is the cord that runs throughout the universe and beyond.

As I share my journal with you, notice the beautiful way Jesus reveals Himself. I encourage you to have an adventure of your own and experience His great love. Your daily encounters with the Lord will probably be different than mine, but they will still be a journey of discovering things about yourself and realizing how lovingly He helps each of us grow.

Here are some simple things that I have learned when I have entered His presence. Maybe this will help you in your time with the Lord. He never intended it to be complicated because He desires to have fellowship with us. We have His word on it–"*Draw near to God and He will draw near to you. . ." James 4:8 NKJV*

1- Sometimes I will begin my time with a time of worship in song, and then other times I will begin by reading my Bible. Then I put everything aside to have my time of prayer with HIM. Simply put, prayer is conversation with God. Talking to Him, who is my best friend.

2- Find a quiet spot. I must find a quiet place so that I am not distracted. I personally enjoy turning on soft instrumental worship music to fill the atmosphere with soft worship. For me, I cannot have music playing with words singing at this time, because my mind will immediately begin to follow along and I am singing instead of listening to His voice.

3- Next, I will begin to just talk to the Lord. I pray about whatever is on my mind. Once again, praying is not complicated. It is simply talking to our greatest love, our best friend, one who knows us better than anyone else. Sometimes I am praying for family and friends, and at other times I am praying for my community and my country.

4- Then, after I have prayed, I quiet myself and simply close my eyes and ask the Lord, "Is there anything that You would want to tell me today, Lord? I am here to listen to

Your heart." Truthfully, taking the time to learn HOW to quiet your own thoughts takes immense effort. It does take time to learn.

5- And then I simply wait. This is probably the most important part. Wait to hear Him. It's as simple as it sounds. Quietly wait. For me, I usually have my eyes closed. It seems to keep distractions down.

6- As I wait, pictures or movies begin to play in my mind's eye–visions. Your experience may differ from mine. Example: Many will experience a place of a creative flow of anointed music springing up in their hearts. For me, it is in visions.

7- I do take time afterward to write down all that I have seen and heard. At this point, I immediately go to God's precious word and hold everything up to it. I would cast aside anything that is contrary to His word. This is a huge lesson that must be learned: knowing the difference between HIS voice, MY own voice, and the voice of the enemy (satan). This is a journey in itself!

I sincerely hope this helps many of you to be able to come into His wonderful presence and find that place where He bids us to "Come and dine". Come! Let's visit with the Lord.

Introduction to Abraham (My Assignment) & Opening My Spiritual Eyes

1 Corinthians 2:9-16
NKJV

9 But as it is written:
   "Eye has not seen, nor ear heard,
   Nor have entered into the heart of man
   The things which God has prepared for those who love Him."

10 But God has revealed them to us through His Spirit. For the Spirit searches all things, yes, the deep things of God.

11 For what man knows the things of a man except the spirit of the man which is in him? Even so no one knows the things of God except the Spirit of God.

12 Now we have received, not the spirit of the world, but the Spirit who is from God, that we might know the things that have been freely given to us by God.

13 These things we also speak, not in words which man's wisdom teaches but which the Holy Spirit teaches, comparing spiritual things with spiritual.

14 But the natural man does not receive the things of the Spirit of God, for they are foolishness to him; nor can he know them, because they are spiritually discerned.

15 But he who is spiritual judges all things, yet he himself is rightly judged by no one.

16 For "who has known the mind of the Lord *that he may instruct Him?" But we have the mind of Christ.*

Matthew 6:6
NKJV

But you, when you pray,
go into your room,
and when you have shut your door,
pray to your Father who is in the secret place,
and your Father who sees in secret will reward you openly.

~Journal Entry Day 1 ~

— The Invitation & Finding Abraham —

I COME INTO a quiet time of rejoicing in the Word. It is worth every moment of our time when we sit and just read His Word. It becomes even richer as we study just a little deeper. Oh, how I love the Word of God; it is so precious to me! I begin to think about how much I'm looking forward to His appearing, His coming again. I have been studying the scriptures about His near return. I've been looking at the passages in 1 & 2 Thessalonians and even delving into parts of the book of Daniel, and oh, my heart is stirred with anticipation.[1] I tell Jesus how much I look forward to His return. "I'm so very anxious to see you, Lord!" I love being in His presence.

After spending time in the Word and praying, I take extra moments to wait on Him. I ask, "Lord, what would You like to say to me? Is there anything today that You want me to know?"

Then I wait in quietness before Him, and the vision opens before me.

His Smile

I see His beaming face, a grin that shows his beautiful white teeth. It's a smile so wide it's almost a laugh. Oh my; it's such a happy and welcoming expression.

The face–I know it to be Jesus. The wind is blowing His hair slightly. It is brown with slightly wavy, soft curls. It isn't shaggy, just beautiful. Everything about Him is so peaceful and loving;

that's what stands out the most about Him. I feel such marvelous love and peace.

He has His hand stretched toward me, looking back, and smiling. SMILING! I am absolutely carried away by His wide grin.

Jesus says, "I can hardly wait to show you. I love you." There is such eagerness in His voice as He says, "I've got so much to show you!"

I can see it in His eyes. They are sparkling with delight, and He has me excited too. His face and smile have me in awe and I find myself totally captivated by what He's saying.

I glance at the Lord again and He is pointing forward now. We are suspended up high, overlooking a vast landscape. Miles and miles of mountains stretch out in front of us in an array of blues, greens, and purples. I refocus on Jesus again, and He is displaying His beautiful, radiant smile. I'm simply overcome with His expression. I can hardly take my eyes off it.

This grin has me a little bewildered. It is so welcoming and loving. Is He smiling at _me_? Really? It seems almost impossible to believe. That beautiful smile is for me.

My voice is a bit shaky as I ask, "Lord, are You smiling . . . at . . . me?" And I'm thinking, *'Is that a happy expression? Are You . . . pleased with me?'* My mind is swirling, slowly taking it in. I could never imagine such a smile. I always think of my mistakes and mess ups and crazy things, and I guess I've never envisioned Him grinning that big at me. I really don't know exactly why. But now, and here . . . His smile makes me feel abundantly approved of and totally accepted and wanted.

He answers my thoughts with, "Of course! Of course, I smile at you. I love you! My heart is bursting with love for you." And He reminds me softly, "I died for you."

Oh, my. Just hearing those words accompanied by that beautiful, amazing smile... I am totally wiped out on this. It wrecks me and I am in tears.

I tell myself, '*I know that I know this.*' I've been a Christian for so many years; I know He died for me. But to hear it from Him, with this incredible expression, brings me to tears. Joyful tears! I have sung 'Jesus Loves Me' my entire life, but this is moving me to my innermost being. I'm now sobbing because I'm so overwhelmed by this kind of love. It absolutely consumes me, pouring through me in waves. His love is enormous.

He knows my thoughts and says, "Don't look backward, just look forward with Me."

I watch as He lifts his hand and points. So much is below and spread out in front of us: a beautiful landscape of mountains, a vivid display of creation. He looks into my eyes and grins again, broadly. I can't imagine a happier, more peaceful expression. That smile absolutely reaches all through me. I feel so approved of and accepted by Him.

The Invitation

Then just in front of Him, I see the backside of a horse. It is a pristine, pure white steed with a beautiful tail that glistens with golden colors. The head lifts and turns slightly, revealing a magnificent golden, sparkling, glistening mane. Oh my... I am amazed. I've never seen anything so striking. Jesus looks back at me and the words just come tumbling out of my mouth, "It's so beautiful." Oh my! And there it is again: that SMILE! It almost takes my breath away. His smile is absolute healing and refreshing. It is radiating all through me. I almost feel reborn again . . . this expression from my Savior has shaken me to the core of my being. I look at the horse, then back to Jesus, and I am scarcely able to comprehend the experience. The sheer beauty of His face and this amazing creature challenge me to absorb it all.

Jesus says, "It's yours." He gives me a moment to digest these words because my eyes are about to pop out from amazement. I can hardly take it all in. "Ride with Me."

My first response is, "Yes Lord! ANYWHERE." Truthfully, I can barely breathe now. But there is no other response to be given. Seeing *this*. "Yes Lord. Yes! Yes! I'm ready for whatever may come. Anywhere, anything, if You are there with me Lord." At the same time, I'm nervously thinking *"I don't know how to ride. Oh, my goodness, I've never ridden a horse before."*

Amazingly, He knows my thought as if I had spoken it out loud. Wow. "I will teach you how." His voice is so reassuring. Now I'm at ease. The Lord of the Universe will instruct me. He is beaming that big smile again and it is so lighthearted, there are just no words to describe it. And the vision fades away.

Reflection and Revelation

To be accepted of HIM is the greatest peace we can ever know. It is so hard here in this life to sometimes find approval or acceptance from people and maybe we bring that insecure feeling into our spiritual lives. We come before God with the feelings left over from our daily lives because we KNOW what we are like. We know our mistakes and failures. How could God, who is so holy and righteous, approve of us? How could He really smile at us with a welcoming, approving, accepting expression that says, *'I love you so very much!'*? But then, we come to this reality, this truth found in His precious word: *"For God So loved the world that He gave His only begotten Son, that whosoever believes on Him will have everlasting life."* [2] There is no love greater than this. Now we come before our loving God covered by the sacrifice of His dear Son. When we search the scripture, we see the fervent heart of God pursuing us, intent on bringing us to Him. Oh, my friends, He does love us so. He really loves us.

— The Invitation & Finding Abraham —

***Jeremiah 33:3
NKJV***

*Call to me, and I will answer you,
and show you great and mighty things
which you do not know.*

~ Journal Entry Day 2 ~

— Opening My Spiritual Eyes —

As I sit in quietness, just soaking in the precious presence of the Lord, I take time to worship. I welcome His presence in our special time and place. And I wait.

Abraham – My Assignment

I see Jesus as He mounts His horse. It is a brilliant white horse; incredibly, even its hooves are white! As they move toward me, I see that He is leading the stunning animal with the gold mane and tail that I saw before. My eyes can scarcely take in its astounding beauty. Jesus then tells me to get on the horse. I'm a bit blown away and shaking my head uncertainly. Uh . . . well, I *am* a bit shy – I've never ridden a horse in my entire life. I'm trying to figure out how to accomplish this task when suddenly, in a split second, I'm up on it. Amazing! I was just on the ground, and in an instant, I'm sitting on its back. What a relief! I rub the side of the horse's head, stroking his gorgeous mane. I mean, he is just too beautiful to resist!

I wonder what his name is. Of course, Jesus knows my thoughts and informs me, "His name is Abraham."

Abraham? I never would've thought 'Abraham.' Maybe I was expecting Lightning or Thunderbolt or Firestorm. You know—horse names. LOL! I laugh as I remember a similar experience Dr. Dale Fife describes in his book, 'Spirit Wind'.[13] In a matter of seconds, I'm considering, *"I don't think I've ever* heard of a horse with that name." Yet here he stands beneath me, this gorgeous animal, Abraham. I could almost shout it out loud, "The Lord says you're mine! Oh, what a fabulous gift you are, Abraham; divinely created, sparkling white and gold. "My Grandaddy's name was Abe, and his dad was Abraham . . ." I'm murmuring out loud. Jesus smiles softly, and I think to myself, *"well, of course He knew that."* Abraham. Abraham. A gift from Jesus. Oh my.

Beginning At the Cross

I notice there is a bridle on my horse and Jesus is holding the reins. I'm good with that. That is not a problem. Nope, not a problem at all. I *definitely want* Jesus to lead!

We start to ride. He is a little out front leading the way. We're suspended in the air extremely high above everything. Scenery goes by quickly and I'm wondering if we are maybe even traveling through time. I'm thinking about what may lay ahead of me, as well as trying to watch where we are going. Landscapes pass quickly beneath us and all around us. After some time, we slow down and stop. Jesus dismounts, so I climb down also, to follow Him.

I can't help but pause just for a moment to touch Abraham's head and that soft gold mane. He is just so breathtaking. Everything the Lord does is beautiful! Each time I see this astounding animal, my whole being is flooded with a feeling of being loved and cared for.

Now I look around trying to see if I know where we are. Nothing really stands out to me at first, but then I begin to recognize a familiar place. I believe we are in Israel. Israel... oh, I love Israel. There are so many Biblical sites that are significant to me, but even when I look around, I can't see anything but this landmark: Golgotha. Only this. Even though I had visited Israel on a tour, this looks a little different. There are no parking lots or buses and cars. Just the landscape and 'the place of the skull'. We are at Calvary. Golgotha. The Cross where Jesus has been crucified. Incredibly, I am drawn to looking at the ground, the soil there. Every tiny grain is magnified like a zoom-in effect.

"I want you to see," I hear Jesus say.

In just a flash, it's as if I have traveled back in time to the day of His crucifixion. I see tears and hear crying from several people. Behind it all is an eerie silence, with no background music (like we are accustomed to hearing in the movies). None. Just these painful voices and sounds. It is such a traumatic time for His disciples and family; I know their hearts are breaking. Of course, I am in tears too. Then I see His heart, breaking as He looks over the earth. Oh Jerusalem... From the cross, he looks out over all the people, knowing who will reject Him, and who will accept. He knows.

There's More

I am processing all of this, taking it all in. Although the wonder of it is moving me beyond anything I've ever experienced, I feel a stirring in my heart that there is something else. I'm certain I'm supposed to comprehend more deeply; I just know it. There is more He wants me to see.

I begin to plead with Jesus. "Please help me, I know I'm supposed to be seeing more. Please help my eyes to see. Anoint them Lord, so I can see."

I look down at the ground because it has captured my total attention. The grains of dirt and sand just got magnified again. I know the Cross was once on this spot. His blood was spilled right here on this very ground where I'm standing, and these granules of sand seem to be the only thing in the world at this moment. I have zoomed in on every tiny piece of grit at my feet.

Ride With Me

Now as I write this, in my mind's eye I can almost see it as I saw in that vision.

The resurrected Jesus I've been riding with is standing nearby, and bends down to pick up some of the dirt from this place where His blood had dripped. He mixes it up in His hands. I can see His face and the dirt in His hands as He comes toward me. I have no idea what is about to happen. He is looking at me and I believe He can see straight through me. His eyes. His face. I cannot move. I will not move. He is looking intently as He places it on my eyes. I remain perfectly still. He covers my eyes with this sand.

Thoughts race through my head. I begin thinking of the story in the Bible in the book of John when Jesus healed a blind man by putting clay on his eyes and told him to wash it off in a pool. I wonder if maybe this is what I'm going to have to do. Maybe I'm going to have to wash in a pool, but just as the thought enters my mind . . .

Holy Spirit Wind

. . . a warm, gentle wind blows across my face and whisks the dirt off my eyes. That wind... I can almost feel it again now. A warm gentle breeze. I just know it is the Holy Spirit. What a blessing. (Even that word seems too small to use because the experience is so wonderful.) What a feeling! "Holy Spirit, I love you!" He is so ever-present. Oh my.

"You will see now." The words are so sure and convincing, I cannot help but believe. Oh my. His voice.

I have the inner knowing that this is not a 'creative' miracle like the man in John chapter 9 of the Bible. Instead, this is a 'revelatory' miracle that comes only through the blood of Jesus and the moving of the Holy Spirit. "Lord, You are so awesome in all Your ways. You are too marvelous for my mind to comprehend." He has touched my eyes so I can see. He wants me to *see*.

Then I hear the song that the Holy Spirit gave me several years ago and I hear Him singing it. Softly at first. Then we sing it together. *He is singing with me!* I hear the Holy Spirit singing. "You could hear the Wind blow – Oooooo. You could hear the Wind blow – Oooooo" (See Appendix A)

The song is about Him, the Holy Spirit, and His awesome presence there at the Cross. This time, singing it with Him and hearing it now, is so different from singing it alone. I can feel every part of that song and I know He feels it too. There is one part in the song that is just a gentle "Ooooo" and hearing His voice as it sings it leaves me completely undone. I am once again in a puddle of tears. He sings so beautifully. I think, 'Lord, you completely melt my heart.'

I hear Him saying, "God so loved–so loved that I came and died for mankind. To have a people. But not just for here. I want you with me. Where I am."

He Has Plans for Us

I can see what He means. He is looking off into a faraway place . . . heaven, our homeland. Our real homeland. To be with Him. *With Him*. Oh my, He WANTS US with HIM! To be with Him in His Kingdom. His Kingdom. He is anxious to have us WITH Him! I can hear excitement in His voice as He repeats, "I can hardly wait for you! I have so much planned!"

I cannot help but feel so loved and wanted! My heart is now beating with excitement too! I see Him as He looks forward and says, "We are going to create many new things together."

I hear it in His voice; He is looking forward to us being with Him. He is truly looking forward to it with great anticipation! My mind is overwhelmed with this kind of love and the knowledge that He is making plans for us to be with Him, to create with Him. It reminds me of when I sit with my sweet grandbabies at our craft table. Except wow! With Him it would encompass the universe and beyond. Oh, my goodness. Oh, I love Him. I cannot help but love Him. His love is just too wonderful to resist. He said *together*! TOGETHER! Let that sink in. I am astounded to say the least. I am overwhelmed. I can barely keep my thoughts together. I am in tears, overflowing with so much peace. Now I am filled with excitement too, thinking of all He is talking about! I hear Him saying, "I love you so. I love you so! I *love* you so!" Over and over and over. And I am in tears again. I never want to lose my ability to hear that. Oh, how He Loves us! OH, HOW HE LOVES US! *Oh, how He loves us*. I feel like shouting it! I just don't think we can fully grasp the depth of love He has for us.

Reflection and Revelation

This time with the Lord is life changing; I will never be the same! I'm so amazed. Jesus extended His hand to me and then toward Abraham. This was the invitation; the invitation to ride. Abraham is going to be key for me in my journey. Later, I receive more revelation about this horse. Abraham represents my walk of faith. This is incredible. Just seeing Abraham is such a blessing. And Jesus holds the reins. He is the Guide of my faith walk. Wow. This revelation came much later after this vision. The Lord let me know that my vision had to be changed to be able to see what was ahead of me. When we journey with the Lord, we will see in the Spirit. Our spiritual eyes must be opened. The carnal, fleshly eyes are not able to see the things of the Spirit. This was a very moving experience. I have had many encounters with the Lord over my lifetime, but this was so different. It seems so much deeper. Oh, just remembering it now, I can almost feel that warm, sweet Spirit blowing over my eyes. I wish I had come sooner Lord. I wish I had come here sooner.

Psalm 51:10
KJV

Create in me a clean heart O God,
and renew a right spirit within me.

Inner Healing
For the Journey Ahead

~ Journal Entry Day 3 ~

— Inner Healing for The Journey Ahead —

"I'M HERE, LORD. Forgive me and cleanse me from anything that is not like You. I'm here waiting to hear You. I've been singing, worshipping, and trying to prepare myself for our time together."

Then I wait before Him.

The Hurts

I see Him. Jesus. He's just in front of me. My heart is overcome with love for Him.

"Are you ready?" He asks.

"Yes, Lord. Whatever You want, I want. Whatever You want." I wonder if we are going somewhere again, but then He turns to me.

"We must begin here first," He says. He is looking at me in quite a simple but serious way. He has a very patient look. I have the feeling this is going to be a learning time. He is looking directly at me and begins to reach toward my heart. *My heart.* I see His hands as they reach toward me, and I can see His face. His expression is soft and patient. He says, "I must do this," with a voice that is tender and caring.

"Okay, Lord. I trust You. I totally trust You." I remain still, not knowing what is about to happen.

He reaches out toward me and begins to pull on something and it starts coming from my heart. It looks like a vine of some kind, rather large and dark with thorns on it. He keeps pulling at it. Ugh! This thing, ugh, oh my! I trust Him; I do! But what in the world? "Please take this thing out of me! I don't like the look of it." And it just keeps coming out. "Lord, please, take it all out! What is this, Lord? Why is it there? Take it out all the way to the roots! Whatever it is, Lord, take it!"

He gently tells me that this thing, this vine with thorns, is the 'hurts.'

"Lord? The hurts?" I ask.

"This is the 'hurts' in your heart." His voice is so soft and not harsh in any way. I swallow hard. I know now, I must let go of old wounds. I cannot keep them. They are so ugly; I don't want to keep them. I didn't even realize I was holding any, but *He* knows and now I want them gone. I'm disgusted. I don't like the look of this dark vine, and I want it to be totally gone.

My attention is drawn then to the thorns on the vine. "What are these thorns?" I ask, "the sharp little things on the vine?"

Jesus replies, "Simply, the longer the hurt stays there, the more pain it will cause. The thorns will grow from these vines, and they cut deep. The hurt then cuts even deeper."

Now I see. The longer the hurt remains, the bigger the offenses will grow and only more and more hurt will come from it. Oh, I see the need is so great to remove every single piece.

"I'm totally submitted to You, Lord. Take them all, Jesus. Please take them. I give them up to you now."

It Hurts to Let Go

I know He knows it hurts to let go of the hurt. It *hurts* to let go. But He continues ever so patiently. I feel nothing but love. Absolute love. I force myself to stay still and let Him work. His face is so gentle, so loving. How could I refuse such a touch? I cannot. I know we must do this before we can ever go anywhere else. It takes time, but I don't resist. I'm anxious for Him to take it ALL away. Every single bit! He is patiently working. I don't sense any anger at all, just a gentle touch that lets me know He wants to help me. It is pure love that I feel. Pure love. There is a time of quietness as He finishes; a very peaceful quiet.

Then He looks at me. "You needed that before we go to the next place."

"Yes. Thank You so much Lord. Oh, thank You. I think of that awful vine and oh, thank You Lord! I can't say 'thank You' enough. Thank You!"

Then I have this crazy thought: what will He do with it? I mean, there He is, having to hold that spiky vine. (And He knows my thought! I will have to get used to Him knowing my thoughts...) He turns and tosses it, and it just disintegrates, vanishing. It is gone. Gone! I can feel it. It is *GONE*. Really gone! Oh. My.

The Next Place

He mentioned the next place. Next place? I am ecstatic! I see Jesus and He has the two horses, His and mine. He mounts His horse and turns to look at me. I almost laugh because I know what He's thinking! How is that? He's watching me as I ponder how to climb up on Abraham's back. I'm determined to mount this horse . . . well, I *am*, uh, getting up on this horse . . . Now, that is a challenge. I kind of chuckle. Oh my! Can I really laugh with Jesus? But I can't seem to help it and a small giggle kind of bubbles out anyway. As I'm looking at Abraham and considering how to accomplish this feat, in an instant, I find myself mounted. Wow. Just wow. I was on the ground, then suddenly I'm on Abraham's back. I just shake my head in sheer amazement.

Voices of Prayer

Jesus is out front, leading the way, and Abraham is following. We're so high; there are landscapes below us and the unfolding scenery is breathtaking. Wisps of my hair as it blows in the wind, my sandal-clad foot, and folds of the robe I wear all catch my eye. I can't help but look down at myself and I'm in shape – not out of shape anymore. (This is a jaw dropping moment here!) Incredibly, the Lord knows my thoughts and says, "I see you as you are in spirit." Now, it's my turn to smile and I do smile big. That is all I'll say about that. LOL!

We continue to ride on, and I glimpse a simple valley below. The deep greens, blues, and yellows are stunningly beautiful. There is a peaceful little settlement in that valley, vibrant with color.

A Planting Of The Lord

As we ride into the village, we approach a small cottage-type house. I see a narrow pathway leading up to the dwelling. Instinctively I know that we are going inside this charming home, set in such a serene little glen. Jesus tells me, "I planted you in a special place, in this peaceful valley. I planted you here."

My understanding is opening. This was my beginning. My mind raced to my parents and my wholesome upbringing. There was no turmoil; it was a loving home. We were normal of course, but we were secure and loved, brought up in church and taught to love Jesus. My Dad was my Pastor. My sisters, brother and I were loved and cared for. Were we perfect? No. But we had a good foundation. I could talk on and on about my sweet childhood. "Oh Lord, thank You so much, Jesus. What a wonderful blessing, thank You so much." Knowing HE had *planted* me there; we are a planting of Him!

Then I look at the cottage. Is this...? Is this my heart? I somehow just know; yes, this is my heart. I swallow hard. Okay. I am steeling myself with resolve. I will not refuse. I will follow the Lord, whatever He needs me to do.

The Prayer Warriors

Jesus and I enter the house into the front room, where I see several of my ancestors. Mama Baker, my great-grandmother, is seated in a rocking chair, and I can hear her praying. My Mother's mother, Grandma Little, is kneeling in front of another chair, earnestly imploring heaven. Mama Chapman, Dad's mother, is calling out to the Lord. Mother and Dad are there, making their heart-felt requests of God. Then I hear a chorus of intercessions from so many special people in my life throughout the years. I can hear their voices ringing out; I recognize them! All of these were and still are powerful, praying people. The most humbling thing of all is that I hear each one of them crying out to God for me. Me. They are interceding for *me*. I can hear those precious voices raised to the Lord on my behalf. The sound of those prayers just rings all throughout my being. Prayer has formed me, surrounded, and kept me. Hearing it is something that absolutely breaks me. I weep. "Thank you, Lord, for these precious warriors! Thank You so much."

My appreciation goes deep. I feel it in my soul. These prayers, and these precious, deeply spiritual family leaders are taking time to lift me up to our heavenly Father. The Lord allows me to listen and absorb all of this for quite a few moments.

It Is Our Turn

"Now, it's up to you," He tells me.

It's my turn to engage in prayer, to sincerely intercede for those I love. "Yes, Lord. My petitions will join these. I will intercede for my children, my husband and family. I will cry out for my friends and those who are lost. I will pray, Lord. Even though I do appeal to You and have done so for years, I now feel the nudging to speak with You about them in an even more intensified manner. My prayers will be different after this experience. Oh, for sure. Prayer will be different.

The Mold

We're still in the cottage and before me, I see what looks like an antique gun. It's a dark bronze color, with a sparkling sheen to it and turquoise embellishments. Upon closer inspection, I notice that it's not solid, but hollow. I examine it repeatedly, and ask Jesus, "What is this? What's it for? It's just a hollow, tin gun. It's not solid like a real gun."

I begin to think it can't be worth much; it's only a shell. I can see what it's supposed to be, but it's not quite there. Yet it's elaborately decorated with these beautiful turquoise gems, so evidently it is of great worth. But what can it possibly be used for? Jesus waits for a while, allowing me to continue to look it over.

"Lord, please teach me," I implore. "What is this?"

He begins to share with me. "This is a form."

"A form?"

"A mold," He clarifies. A MOLD! Of course, a mold! I know what a mold is! Now I wait to see exactly what that means. A mold. What is it for? A mold for what? I can see it's in the shape of a gun of sorts. But what is it for?

"I created this mold. I chose the substance and poured it into the mold to form the weapon. Likewise, I have made you. You are a weapon that I have formed. I will pour the substance of My choice into you, and provide the ammunition that will flow from you. I will guide you, and aim you in the direction that I need. And I will be the One Who releases the flow from this weapon. I choose the timing. I choose the target. You are my weapon."

Wow. The weapon is me. The ammunition is His Word that He downloads into me. This is astounding; a mind-blowing moment for me. I look again at the mold. This mold. I know He is filling me with His Word, guiding and equipping me. It's so humbling to know that He is molding me, filling me. "Lord, fill me! Fill me!"

These Are Not Life to You

Then I look up and it's as if I can see through the roof of the cottage. The ceiling is there, but I can see through it, almost as if it is clear glass. Blue sky and trees show above it. Some of the trees are gorgeous and green, but others are dead, dry, gray-looking and leafless. Those are the ones that catch my attention, and I ask Jesus, "What are these dry trees?"

He simply replies, "leave the things that are dry behind. Discard them; they are not life to you. If there is no life in them, remove them."

The dry, dead trees look so out of place with the fresh green ones against that gorgeous blue sky. I said, "Lord please help me to do that. Help me to see what is dry and dead and help me to get rid of it." I'm so anxious now to remove the dead and dry things; so very anxious. It's time to remove them. There is much for Jesus to work on with me and I'm thinking there will be even more as time passes. I'm so very thankful for His work in my life.

My heart longs to see more, but there's nothing further at the moment. Still, I don't want to leave; I'd rather stay here in His presence. Even though this has been a time of revealing and working, I still want to be right here! When He is changing things in me, it is the most incredible experience of feeling loved and cared for.

And then, as if He is soothing my heart, He says, "Little one, enough for this time". He called me 'little one'! My heart is once more warmed, and I feel so loved and cherished I can barely find words to describe it. Suddenly, we are outside of the cottage. "Let's take a ride." I know this time is just for pure enjoyment. Is that possible? I'm learning so much.

Again, we are on our horses. Oh my! The beauty of the ride, the sheer magnificence of the horses, the Wind in our hair stir me. I know this Wind, this precious Wind. "Holy Spirit, You are here, moving all around." We ride over the landscape until it fades.

Reflection and Revelation

My time in His presence this day was pretty intense. It all revolved around preparing me to be used by Him. Healing past hurts in my heart, allowing me to hear my family's prayers over me, revealing how He was molding me as a weapon to be used, and teaching me to be aware of the influences around me, were all part of His plan to get me ready. When Jesus began to pull the hurts from my heart, I was amazed that they were even there. The dark vine surprised me and I learned that the thorns were the offenses that can grow out of the hurts. But how awesome it is that He sees what we do not see. He knew I needed this. I am so thankful for His healing. As we ponder this, Jesus took our sins and our hurts on the cross. Were our hurts, all those painful vines, were they indeed His crown of thorns? Oh, friends, our precious Savior is so worthy of all our adoration.

There was such a wonderful peace that came after that. Time in His presence will change us. I pray, "Lord, don't leave me today like you found me this morning. Change me every day to be more like You."

I also see now that the dry trees represent the things that are not life to me; I'm left with a dryness in my spirit if I allow them or spend time there. These are the dry trees that must not be a part of my life. I must be vigilant and guard my heart and mind. The trees could symbolize people, or they could mean influences in my mind, since I can see them through the ceiling of my house. I've gained a new awareness about guarding my mind against any thoughts that are not life to me. I need to be on guard. "Lord, I present myself to You, for whatever You need and whatever Your heart desires."

Matthew 6:9-13
KJV

9 – After this manner therefore pray ye: Our Father which art in heaven, Hallowed be thy name.

10 – Thy kingdom come. Thy will be done in earth, as it is in heaven.

11 – Give us this day our daily bread.

12 – And forgive us our debts, as we forgive our debtors.

13 – And lead us not into temptation, but deliver us from evil: For thine is the kingdom, and the power, and the glory, forever. Amen

---

Titus 3:4-5
NKJV

4 But when the kindness and the love of God our Savior toward man appeared,

5 not by works of righteousness which we have done, but according to His mercy He saved us,

through the washing of regeneration and renewing of the Holy Spirit.

~ Journal Entry Day 4 ~

— Deeper Healing of the Past —

The Renewing

My time with the Lord begins with prayer. I walk out to my porch, quoting the Lord's Prayer over my family and community. This recitation has so much more meaning to it now. I take my time coming into my special place with the Lord.

"I love You so much Lord! Thank You for all that You are to me. I am here for You to speak to me, or whatever you want." And I wait quietly before him.

When Jesus enters my sight, He's holding an object in His hand. As I watch, He places the object inside a yellowish gold bag with a long strap, and folds a flap over the opening. He then hangs the shoulder bag around my neck, indicating that I am to keep it. Of course, I will.

The Lord is astride His horse and Abraham walks up beside me. Jesus looks back at us and says with a bit of a grin, "you know you're going to learn to mount."

I'm skeptical, and think, 'Oh my...okay...help me, Lord!' Once again I start out standing on the ground and suddenly find myself effortlessly seated on Abraham's back. Whew! My, how I love this creature. He is such a comfort now.

I notice that my clothing is different today. It's not a flowing garment, but simple light brown, loose-fitting pants, and a loose-fitting shirt.

Jesus starts us out on a rather narrow trail that appears to descend downward. Immediately, I wonder if we are continuing our previous journey from Golgotha and heading toward Jerusalem. But no, this road follows alongside a massive landscape and He lets me know we are continuing forward. Our trail gradually narrows as we ride through a woodsy area, until it is almost a simple footpath. I glimpse a narrow bridge ahead that appears only wide enough for a man to walk across; it is suspended over a small stream. A feeling of uncertainty comes upon me as I consider the fact that we are on horses, and the span is small.

Jesus (as you know He would) assures me it is perfectly safe. "Okay, I trust you Jesus." So, we travel on.

The trees are getting taller, the woods thicker. Ahead I see a log cabin that seems very small. We ride right up to it and dismount. Jesus looks at me and says, "We're going in."

The Fireplace & the Rocking Chairs

He pushes the door open into a small room. There is a fire burning in the hearth with two wooden rocking chairs in front of it. The fire is lighting the room and it is so warm. Jesus looks at me with a gentle but serious expression on His face. We sit in the rocking chairs, and He is watching me. As I gaze into the fire, memories begin flooding my mind; hurtful events that happened long ago. I never told anyone about what went on but felt ashamed of myself because if I had told, others may not have suffered. I was so young at the time and didn't know what to do.

"The shame you feel is not from Me, it's from the enemy." He looks back toward the fire with a grim expression. I somehow know as those memories are playing in my mind, He is seeing the past too. He knows. My sweet Jesus knows.

"Take it away." I feel anger begin to burn in me. "Lord, please take it away." I know He can see the anger. "Lord, please help me." I am struggling with these emotions, and He sees it.

Refreshing of the Water of the Word

My Savior takes the yellow bag from my shoulder and tells me to look inside. I reach in and pull out a bottle. It is a large, antique glass bottle which Jesus holds for me to take a drink. As I obey, I can immediately feel it flowing through my body.

"This is your refreshing," He says. "It refreshes and renews your mind. My Word in *John 4:14* declares *'whoever drinks of the water that I shall give him will never thirst. But the water that I shall give him will become in him a fountain of water springing up into everlasting life.' NKJV* This water of the Word is springing up new life in me. *New life. Everlasting life.* I can feel the life-giving source flooding my whole being.

Renewing of the Mind

Jesus tenderly brushes hair away from my forehead and places His hand there. With a gentle stroke, He murmurs, "a renewing of your mind."

The scripture immediately comes to my mind about "renewing of the mind" in Romans 12. [4]

My mind is being renewed.

"You will not see this the same after today. You will see differently." The phrase 'broken people hurt people' has such meaning to me now. I've heard it before, but new understanding is growing in me. Jesus had been broken, so He knows my pain. Then there is a gentle atmospheric change all around me.

"I release this, Jesus. I give it all to You." The words 'you will see it differently' are ringing repeatedly in my spirit now, and fresh understanding comes. With a renewed mind comes a new vision that has been refreshed in the Spirit realm. I pray, "Lord, every day. Renew my mind every day!"

Romans 12:2 NKJV declares, "And do not be conformed to this world, but be transformed by the renewing of your mind, that you may prove what is that good and acceptable and perfect will of God."

We sit now in front of the fire, and it is warming me all the way to my toes. I think this is the healing presence of the Holy Spirit. This fire is healing. We sit and soak it in for a long time before we move to leave.

The Decree

As we get to the door, He looks at me with just a bit of a nod and comments, "we won't return to this place. We won't come back here." The words hang in the atmosphere for a while. As we are going out the door, I'm aware that I have the bag with me. I am going to need this water of refreshing in days to come. We're on our horses now, and Jesus is leading us on the path again. He is just in front of me, and my attention is drawn to the fact that He's wearing the King's crown on His head and a royal robe flows from His shoulders. This is the first time I have seen Him wearing this attire. The Almighty King of kings is astride His magnificent white horse, and I am with Him. I only see Him from the back now, but it is still an awe-inspiring moment. Deep reverence settles over me as I reflect on the fact that there has been a decree from the King made over me today. I am in awe of His presence and the feeling in the atmosphere as we leave the small cabin. I will not speak now. I'll just follow close behind Him in absolute honor and respect, remaining quiet as we travel. I'm following the King, and He has decreed freedom over me.

Reflection and Revelation

It had to be this way. I had to let go of the trauma from my past. Isn't it just like our sweet Lord to help us heal and move on? We don't even realize that we are being held back until He begins to deal with us about it. "Thank You, Lord, for the freedom that I feel. Thank You so much."

He is getting me ready. What is ahead of me? I'm looking forward with great anticipation for our next journey.

Zephaniah 3:17
NKJV

*The Lord your God in your midst,
The Mighty One, will save;
He will rejoice over you with gladness,
He will quiet you with His love,
He will rejoice over you with singing."*

Learning to Move In the Heavenlies

~ Journal Entry Day 5 ~

— Learning To Move In The Heavenlies —

I'M WAITING IN His presence, in the quiet place. I 've spent my time praying and now I'm waiting before Him. I simply ask if there is anything He wants me to see or to know today, and I take the time to wait.

Jesus is standing beside me, and Abraham waits ahead of me. My horse is wearing a saddle. It looks ordinary; nothing really stands out about it. Jesus is hanging a bag on the saddle horn, then placing something in it. I remember the gold bag that held the water of the word for me. Without a doubt, I need this Word with me. I know that whatever He is loading into the bag, we will be needing it. I am so touched that He is taking such care of me. Then I wonder why is a saddle necessary when I've been riding without one? Perhaps it's needed to carry such things.

Suddenly, I notice Abraham's hooves. Oh, my goodness! I hadn't paid attention to them before. They're gold and the bottoms sparkle with a gold sandy substance. Gold? Gold sand? Gold *dust*... Of course! It hits me. He walked on the streets in heaven. Gold... streets of gold. My mind is blown again.

The Veiled Place

The course ahead of us leads through thin, filmy blue veils. Peacefully, gently blowing in the Wind, they appear almost alive. Elegant and soft, the waving sheers invite me into that space beyond. And oh my, I know that sweet, gentle Wind; the Holy Spirit is beckoning. I know we'll be going through the moving curtains. The path ascends slightly and then out of sight beyond the veils. I look at Abraham and then Jesus.

"You're going too, right?"

Jesus assures me, "You can trust Abraham. He has traveled this pathway many times."

At that moment, I'm confident that Jesus is accompanying us. We wait as Abraham walks down the trail alone, ahead of us. Shortly he returns through the veils. with two people riding on him. They dismount, and I catch only a momentary glimpse of them. In the brief sighting, I notice one of them is a young man with a small hat. It is only a momentary glance, and they are not introduced to me, so evidently that must be for another time. "I am content with whatever You want to show me Lord."

Jesus, Abraham, and I head toward the trail. As we approach the beginning of the veil path, the glorious stallion pauses at the entrance. There, we leave a set of cylinders or vessels, jars or perhaps canisters, all tied together with a woven cord, then begin our journey through the filmy curtains. The trail is rather narrow, and the veils occasionally brush lightly against us.

I experience an overwhelming sense of awe; these veils are so significant. I feel like we are passing through the heavens as the wispy curtains are gently blown by the Wind. At times a veil slightly flows over me as I pass by it, just a soft, wispy touch.

'Yes, Lord,' I muse. 'The heavens are veiled and only You can lead us through this vast space.' Oh, it's so magnificently glorious to be here and see this.

The Ancient Book

A massive book is suspended over our pathway up ahead. It's ancient and heavy, elaborately embossed with gold. The enormous volume opens, and shooting upward out of it are the cosmos: the stars... the heavens... clouds... colossal space. All are radiating out of the immense tome.

"You need to see the Beginning."

The Beginning. . . I'm seeing the Creation. I have the incredible feeling that *all* of the heavens, and everything in them, are watching as Creation is recorded. Jesus is writing in the tremendous volume and the cosmos is springing forth out of it. And He's singing. The sound is overwhelming: He sings as He creates. All of heaven watches and listens with great anticipation while Jesus is here. Every element burst into song with Him as they behold this great endeavor. The experience is almost too much for me, the joy far greater than I can even say. 'Thank you, Lord, for preparing me,' is the grateful thought from my heart.

Jesus sings a happy love song as He gazes at this tender Creation. It doesn't seem to be work to Him at all, but instead, a joyful interplay between Him and His awesome design. My Savior sings and creates and the entire universe arises, springs up. The heavenlies are being birthed in His wondrous time here. He speaks, and it's a song. He utters a word, and everything responds to His voice. *Everything.* The entirety of the universe, the earth in all its splendor, all that exists comes into being because of His voice. He's the Word. The Word sings to it all. The song... oh my!

I can't help but feel so adored and cherished, knowing that He loves every moment of creating the universe, creating us. It's almost more than I can imagine. Oh, it makes me love Him so much more. I'm overflowing with tremendous love for our Savior. He's so awesome and good and loving. There isn't one thing about Him that's not good.

I look to see just a part of His creation, a small sample of this greatness. My eyes light upon the gorgeous mountains. Did you know? He walked through these mountains!

"There are many creatures that you've never seen," I hear Him saying.

Creatures I've never seen... I can sense that He's genuinely excited to get to show me and all of us these creatures in the heavens. It gives me such a great longing for heaven. My homeland...

Reflection and Revelation

We're citizens of heaven, just pilgrims here. This world is not our home. We're natives of another Land. *Philippians 3:20 NKJV says, "For our citizenship is in heaven, from which we also eagerly wait for the Savior, the Lord Jesus Christ."*

The gentle Wind blowing through the veils is the Holy Spirit. He's opening that heavenly realm of vision to us. It's only through Him that we understand any of the things of God. He's our Teacher and guides us in the truth. I'm amazed at the Holy Spirit and His awesome ability to teach us by showing us His Word. Once again, I'm in awe at the absolute love of our God as He forms us. What love! In my mind I'm thinking, 'Is the ancient book His journal? Is it His record in the heavens, the eternal recording?' And I must ask Jesus about the canisters... I feel so small. There's so much to learn. So very much.

John 1:1-5
KJV

In the beginning was the Word,
and the Word was with God,
and the Word was God.
2 The same was in the beginning with God.
3 All things were made by Him;
and without Him was not anything made that was made.
4 In Him was life; and the life was the light of men.
5 And the light shineth in darkness;
and the darkness comprehended it not.

~ Journal Entry Day 6 ~

— The Heavenlies Contain His Story —

In my special 'quiet time' place, I worship the Lord and try to calm my spirit and soul. I feel concern that I won't ever enjoy His presence again and tell Him how very anxious that makes me feel. Yes, I realize that He knows my thoughts . . . I'm determined to settle myself down, to just worship and enjoy my awesome Savior. So, I wait for a bit of time, quietly.

When I see His face, I weep with relief. Jesus's expression is so warm and loving. Is there anything else like it? Ten thousand times no!

"Oh, how I love You, Lord! Oh, I love you! It's enough just seeing Your face and knowing You're here."

"My beloved, I will never leave you. I'm always here."

His assurance totally wipes me out. Soaking that in, I'm in tears again.

"Thank You, Lord. I can't say it enough. Thank You, thank You, thank You, thank You. I must stay here for a while. Thank You."

Opening into the Heavenlies: A Portal

I see Abraham. Jesus walks up to my glorious companion and joyfully strokes the side of his head.

"I have many." He speaks.
"Many?" I respond.

He strokes him again. "Many," He says, looking into a faraway place.

Jesus has many of these magnificent horses. *Many.* I know in my mind that He's looking toward the heavenlies. Heaven. Our future home. I look at Abraham and wonder if we are going to travel somewhere today.

"Not yet," the Lord tells me. "Let's sit for a moment."

"Anything Lord. Anything." I reply.

We walk for a piece, then stop on the edge or side of something cloudy. It seems as if we're sitting on a ledge, high and suspended above the cosmos, looking over into another dimension. Space and all the stars are spread out in front of us. I'm blown away in awe of it all; I can barely take it in. As I gaze around me, overcome by the vastness and beauty, Jesus smiles. In my small vocabulary, I attempt to tell Him how beautiful it is. The glittering stars... the immense space. Deep space is stunning in its beauty. Galaxies are suspended and glimmering before us.

Glancing at Jesus as He surveys His boundless creation, again I see Him smile. In His eyes I recognize a genuine love for all that's displayed before us. Pointing at a small blue ball suspended in this infinite realm, He indicates that I should take notice. A small blue ball... Suddenly, I'm astounded. It's Earth. *Earth.* I'm certain my eyes are huge and I'm shaking my head in sheer wonderment.

"Oh Lord, I've only seen pictures of this in books."

The sight is too wonderful for me to speak further. He then draws us near to it.

"My creation."

He smiles, and very lovingly shows me Earth in its original condition. Oh, the colors! The splendid grandeur is all the beauty I've ever seen, magnified a hundred times.

Jesus hesitates. "It's before the Fall." The word 'Fall' is slightly quieter than the rest.

My emotions rise and I find myself longing to say, 'I'm so sorry.' I want to sob because I know we're all part of that sin.

"See Earth as it was in the Beginning." With a determined expression, He declares, "It will be like this again, and even better. *It will be.*"

I believe every word of it. Just hearing Him declare the future, I believe every word. There's a feeling I have, almost like a little child standing beside my father and holding my head high because of what he says. I want to yell it out to everyone. It's easy to spend more time to behold the beauty of Earth: the trees, the grass, the flowers, the meadows; all breathtakingly colorful. Up ahead I see a waterfall feeding a stream and it flows through the place where we stand. As we walk nearer, I think, 'no picture compares with this.'

Sheer Adoration for Our Creator

The waterfall is so gorgeous, sparkling clear and soft. Is it possible for water to be soft? Well, of course it is! I don't know how, but it is. Jesus leans over the pool and so do I, compelled to put our hands in the crystal-clear water. And then of all things, He splashes it, and laughs, astonishing me. We laugh together, gleefully. Oh, it's just a little splash. That incredible smile is absolute healing to my innermost soul. Seeing a happy Jesus is the most marvelous therapy I've ever experienced. Then He starts tapping the water with His hand, His palm open on the top of the water, kind of slapping it softly. The water bounces with little waves radiating out from it. Then fish begin to appear: schools and schools of them. All colors and all kinds swarm around Him. Jesus dips His hand in a little deeper, up to His elbow, and the fish seem to rush in to caress His hand. I'm about to lose my composure altogether, seeing this reaction. Fish of all varieties and hues, small ones and big ones, dolphins and even sharks come up to His hand to touch Him, to caress Him. They all want to touch Him! All types of fish swim up to Him. I'm watching with pure ecstasy as this scene unfolds before me. They adore Him!

He smiles (oh my! that smile...) and says "They know my touch. They were created by Me."

Oh, what glorious love. He loves them. I can't explain this love. It's greater than I've ever imagined; unfathomable. This is so moving that it makes me weep with joy. I'm so overcome I just can't help it.

His Treasure

We leave the waterfall and begin to walk through this beautiful place. It's rich with lush green grass, the smell of fresh clean air, the trees in all their splendid color. In the distance, I see two people and instinctively know who they are.

Jesus sees them and says, "My treasure. My treasured creation."

He's talking about Adam and Eve. The love and joy He felt as He created them, while singing a love song, is so obvious. He put His heartbeat in them. I can touch my heart and know He put it there. The two people are behind a misty, transparent veil of some kind, so I don't see them in perfect clarity, but at a distance. If they're unclothed, it's not noticeable.

He Taught Them to Dance

Adam and Eve are walking and talking. I can hear them laughing and just having fun surrounded by this glorious place. And then I see them dance. Yes, dance. They're dancing and twirling around and having a wonderful time.

"I taught them to dance," Jesus informs me with such a loving voice; He's so delighted.

Wonderment must show all over my face because He has a sweet smile and repeats, "I taught them to dance. They're dancing to the song I made for them".

I watch Adam and Eve dance and can hear His heart in them. I think I'm about to explode! This is so lovely, so amazingly beautiful. My mind is reeling with what it must've been like to have been there. My heart is filled with a longing to be with Him, a longing for that day when I see Him as He fully is.

Suddenly I hear and see something I can't quite identify. The sound of the dance has changed. The Lord indicates that it's time to leave. Somehow, I know what's coming, and a bit of sadness is in my heart. Abraham is at my side and brushes up against me with his head. So, we begin our journey again. Jesus is leading us down a route that goes through this incredible place, a little path through the trees that overlook the stream and the meadow. We ride through the gloriously-colored trees, and then through the veils, the lovely veils. I can't contain myself this time; it's more than I can take. I'm weeping. I can't contain it. It's not a sad weeping, but an overflowing emotion, because of His great goodness.

Reflection and Revelation

And as I write this, I'm weeping again. My vocabulary isn't large enough to describe something so incredible and amazing. But I'm trying to relate what I experienced. It's so astounding that Jesus would slip back the curtain and allow me to see just a tiny bit of the magnificence of the Beginning. While I was in the vision, I could see His total love and adoration for all His creation, but especially Mankind. I think that's His message to me in this day. He loves us. He loves us so much. Having the opportunity to see just a small part of His greatness in the universe brings me to a place of reverence and awe like no other. He's the Ruler of this universe and beyond. He is God Almighty, the Master of it all, and He calls *us* His treasured creation. His treasure! Oh, His love is so overwhelming. Oh my...

As I've read over the journal entries again and again, revelation comes to me about Abraham, in the meaning of his name: father of many. Many! Oh, my goodness. Jesus said to me "I have many!"

Colossians 1:16-17
NKJV

*16 For by Him all things were created
that are in heaven a that are on earth, visible and invisible,
whether thrones or dominions or principalities or powers.
All things were created through Him and for Him.
17 And He is before all things,
and in Him all things consist."*

~ Journal Entry Day 7 ~

— He is Far Beyond the Heavenlies —

OH, HOW I'VE longed to return to this place. My Father knows how I yearn for time in His presence. There are things we must do to continue in this life. But I find myself in a rush to get back here, to Him, to His presence, to be accepted and approved and loved by Him. I love Him so. I can't describe the overwhelming love I feel just to be near Him.

"I'm here Lord. I wait for You."

Doorways in the Heavenlies

Large white double doors are swinging open. Jesus is beside these doors and His hand is extended toward the dark space beyond. It's the dark midnight blue of the cosmos. When I look at Jesus, the hesitancy I feel vanishes immediately. 'Wherever You lead Lord, I will follow,' is my first thought.

We start to walk through the doorway and immediately a throttle appears, like one that I've seen on a big ship, and Jesus has His hand on it.

He pushes it forward as far as it will go and says, "Full throttle ahead."

We begin to move through this heavenly place. It truly feels like we're on a ship. Jesus's hair is blowing back a bit from the movement. We float in dark outer space, kind of slicing through it, almost like it's water we're parting. Looking underneath us, I can see light: brilliant light full of yellows and golds. But we don't stop to look at any of it. We're moving toward a specific destination ahead.

I see the sun and watch Jesus take it in His hand, holding and turning it. Incredible. He rotates it and says, "I cause it to shine. I decided when it began, and I decide when it will cease. No one and nothing will determine that except Me."

I can't help but say, "Nothing exists without You, Lord."

I find myself saying it over and over until it hits me like a ton of bricks: nothing exists *outside* of God. There's nothing outside Him. *Nothing* outside Him. I could shout this from the highest mountain. In Him all things exist. *In* Him. All things. This immense space, this cosmos, exists *in* Him. Not outside of Him. All things. And then all things are coming to Him.

He says "I'll bring all things to Me. No one can speed it up or push Me, and no one will hold Me back. I determine the finality of all things."

"Yes, Lord!" I ask Him ever so quietly about intercession. "Lord, when we intercede, how does it affect things? How does prayer make a difference?"

He responds, "I stir the intercessors' hearts and give the inspiration to pray. My decree is to pray that My will be done. True intercessors hear My heart and pray My will."

I hear His emphasis on *true* intercessors.

The Lake of Fire

Then I look ahead and see a gigantic, circular place opening in front of us. In the middle of this dark cosmos is a swirling fire of yellows, reds and oranges. A large black area in the center grows red. As I watch, it begins glowing and rolling and now it looks like the inside of a live volcano or volcanic lake. Oh, my goodness. Is it what I'm thinking it is?

"Lord, is this...?"

My heart stirs. Jesus turns to me, and it seems like He's holding back a curtain of sorts so I can see a portion of the scene. I know He has somehow cloaked it a bit because I can't bear it otherwise. There's a fiery lake and I hear the low, guttural moans, groans of misery that are beyond even a scream. Oh, I know the screams are there, but at this moment, this is what I hear and see. Oh my, it's horrible. Tears are streaming down my Savior's face. Tears. I weep with Him. My heart is breaking. I cry and cry.

I hear Him as He says, "I didn't create this for men."

His face... Oh, the look on His precious face as He says this. The pure emotion of it all is my complete undoing.

"They open the door by their obedience to satan. It was meant for him."

The Plea

He pleads with me, "Please, Kathy! Please keep them from here. Please help Me keep them out of this place."

I'm trembling and tears are flowing. No one should choose to come here. No one. I now see men who have not accepted Christ. They've died and are looking at this horror before them. The realization hits them as they stand here, that this can't be avoided now. It's final, and that first moan comes out of them. It's awful. Heart rending. That first awareness... I can't describe their reaction.

It hurts Jesus to see it. He says, "From Creation, I made the way out. From Creation, the Beginning, I made the way of escape. The foundation was laid; I paid the way."

As He says this, I'm thinking of His death, His crucifixion. I know. Jesus is the only way. The only way to heaven, the only way to escape this place. His way is salvation.

Slowly, we back out of the view of hell in a sobering, somber silence. I can't speak, and Jesus is quiet also. I'm overcome by it all and Jesus knows it.

He breaks the silence with, "Ride with Abraham."

And amazingly, he's here. A true comfort, this precious jewel, a cherished gift from Jesus. The ride helps to calm my heart. We're going back through space, then the veils. Just as we exit the filmy curtains, I see the canisters that were left outside this entry. They're being filled. What? What am I seeing now about these? What are they? What's the reason? He lets me ponder for a bit. Then I see and understand. They're being filled outside this veil with a substance from within the veil. They are being filled with what we've just seen and heard. Even with the canisters loaded onto Abraham, there's plenty of room for me because I see my place on his back. Oh my… we are to carry the filled containers.

"Abraham, help me walk by faith."

I will go wherever the Lord leads and pour the containers out wherever and to whomever I'm led. I'm shaken, totally undone. Wrecked.

Reflection and Revelation

Nothing exists outside of God. Get that! There's nothing outside of Him. *Nothing outside of Him*! In Him all things exist. In Him. All things exist. In Him.

If you could only see His face as we looked into hell and heard the torment of those who chose to reject His gift of salvation.

I have a more determined heart now to reach as many as I can to keep them from going to an eternal torment. To carry the wonderful salvation message is a great privilege and honor. We're representing our Savior, Jesus. How can we not tell others, especially those we love, about Him? How can we not tell them how to escape this eternal judgment? We have the keys to the Kingdom, the key to eternal life and we must share it. We must.

In Him all things exist. *In* Him. This is too marvelous to even comprehend with my finite mind. Do we even have a small understanding of how great our God is? Do we know His vastness? Is it even possible for us to grasp the enormity of it all? I wonder. Knowing as much as we can know, I put my total trust for my future in His great big hands. He holds it all. ALL.

(Incidentally, I do know it would probably be proper to capitalize the name of satan but somehow, I just can't give him that proper title. I guess that's silly of me, but I want it to be small case. Small. Insignificant. And only Jesus, our precious Lord deserves that honor. Every reference to Him is capitilized)

Revelation 4:5
KJV

*"And out of the throne
proceeded lightnings and thunderings and voices. . ."*

The Significance of Worship

~Journal Entry Day 8~

— Worship and Revival —

EVERY MORNING I take time to pray for all my family, my friends, and my church.

"Lord, bring Your kingdom to them, and them into Your kingdom. I worship You because You're so good. I've looked forward to our time together. Here I am now; I wait before You. I wait in Your goodness and in Your presence."

Dancing with Lightning

I see Abraham, noticing his beautiful head, and that glorious mane of gold. Looking down at myself, I realize that my clothing is once again the flowing, breezy robe I've worn before. I'm barefooted and can feel the ground under my feet. When I mount my stunning horse, he turns his head one way and I see his magnificent mane. Then he turns another way, revealing his muscled, arching neck. He is so striking. This gift from Jesus is almost too captivating to describe.

"Thank You so much, Jesus. Thank You so much!"

Suddenly the stallion breaks into a gallop. After we have run for a while, I begin to see flashes of light beneath our feet. Bright streaks are shooting under and around us. We slow to a stop, and I climb down, almost gliding. This is different... Bolts of lightning and dazzling flares are all around. Abraham begins to move in time with the lightning, his feet connecting with the glimmering streaks. WOW! It is astounding just to watch him as his hoof steps land precisely with the flashes. Then in a striking move, he rears up. The brilliant white horse is huge when he stands on his hind legs like that. What a magnificent creature he is. The impressive animal rears again and twirls with the flashes of light all around him. Abraham is dancing. Oh, my goodness... He's dancing with the lightning. This is incredibly amazing to watch.

Transformation

Then everything changes and there is fire. The flames start on the horse's shimmering mane and then totally engulf him. He is a stallion on fire! His bold head is held high, and I can't take my eyes off him. Unbelievably, I'm instructed to ride.

"Ride? *Really*? Ride?"

"Yes." Comes the simple reply from the Lord.

"Anything for you Lord! Anything."

So, I obey, and yes, I'm mounted on this blazing, fiery horse. The flames start blowing all through me, filling me up without doing any damage. Words will not come for this experience.

Bringing the Fire

We ride again, and what a journey it is. Flames are flowing from us. Oh my...

"Tell me, Lord. Tell me!" My mind is clamoring with the need to know everything about what is happening. "What is this? What does it mean?" My mind can't keep up; it's too wonderful to behold.

"Flames of revival." He replies.

I can see the trail of fire burning behind Abraham. We ride fast and furiously. Next, we stop and I dismount for a moment so I can compose myself.

Rocks and Thorns

A shovel appears; first the handle and then the entire shovel, smoothing the ground. Then I see a rake, a steel one, raking through the soil, sifting out rocks.

"Tell me, Lord. What am I seeing here?"

Jesus tells me in a voice that is instructive, one of a teacher speaking to a student. "I planted the seeds of revival, but rocks held it back and thorns choked it. I planted precious seeds. Now again I plant the seeds. Keep the rocks and thorns out."

"What hinders the seeds from growing?"

"Rocks that won't move." He says.

I pray, "Lord, remove the hindrances. Help us to move with You."

He then tells me more. "Thorns that choke are the things that withhold."

"Lord, please help us all to loosen our grip, our chokehold, our unwillingness to change, and let the seeds grow."

"The fire will come."

Immediately I think of Abraham, my horse on fire. I wonder; is this a revival? The word 'revival' almost seems too small a word for what I've seen. Is this the transformation? Renewal? Is it revival? I'm trying so hard to understand, but it feels as if there's more to this.

"It's the Church as it's supposed to be, when it arises."

Oh, my goodness. I must soak a few moments in that. The fire is the Church as it's meant to be when it arises. The concept just flat out hits me: *what the Church is supposed to be.*

"Oh, Lord, let the Church arise! Lord, let that fire come and transform the Church so that she arises and comes to what you have ordained for her to do in this season."

Church, arise!

— Worship and Revival —

Reflection and Revelation

A few weeks later, I gained more insight into the lights that were flashing around us: they are the Word from the Almighty. God declares the Word and it goes out like lightning. Abraham represents my walk of faith, and his feet are making contact and connecting with God's Word. The flashes of light were coming from the Throne of God. Thunders and lightnings are His voice. Our God was declaring His Word in the flashes of light.[5]

Abraham danced in this Word and then was transformed into the Flame of Revival.

"Lord, send this Word that we may hear and believe and experience the flame of Your glory."

Declarations from the Lord are imparted to the Church, His people, and when we connect to these declarations in our walk of faith, we are transformed into the flaming force that He can use in revival.

"Oh Lord, we must connect."

Let's keep our spiritual ears alert to the true declarations of the Lord as they come forth in this day. Only truth will bring us to this point; untruths, lies and deceptions will not. We keep our spiritual hearts and ears guarded, but we must shield them even more in this season. As children of the Almighty God, we know His voice. We protect ourselves and will not be misled, even in this hour of great deception. We must stay close to His heart. Let the Church hear Him and be transformed and then arise. Let the Church be what it's supposed to be in this earth.

Psalm 141:2
NKJV

Let my prayer be set before you as incense;
the lifting of my hands as the evening sacrifice.

~ Journal Entry Day 9 ~

Worship in Pureness —

I am making this as an extra entry today to make it easier to separate. It is a separate experience but happened on Day 8.

I HAVE SPENT my time in His presence and experienced such an awesome revelation about connecting with God's word and I start to get up from my quiet time. I am thinking the time with Him is over, but I feel a tugging of the Holy Spirit, I will not pull away from His gentle tug, and Holy Spirit is pulling me back into His presence. I obey this feeling to linger a little longer because I know He has more to share with me. So, I sit back down, and I take more time to listen intently. I wait quietly before the King of kings.

The Climb

Jesus has a towel draped across His arm. He leads me by the hand to a solid rock mountain, an immense rock cliff which I am seeing that we're going to climb. My Savior simply hops up on several toe holds and one by one shows me exactly where to place my feet. (I'm wearing shoes this time.) For every single step, He guides my feet and hands as we scale the rock cliff together. I'm amazed; I've never climbed a rock wall, but Jesus makes it so simple. All I must do is place my hands and feet exactly where He says, and up we go. We're almost at the top now. Jesus reaches back to take me by the hand and hoists me over the ledge at the top, lifting me up for the last leg of the climb. When we reach the top of the mountain, it's evening and the sunset colors peep through the trees. The sun isn't all the way down but casts beautiful hues across the sky.

The Altar

I see what I think is a table, but as I look more closely, I'm shocked to learn that it's not. The impact is so powerful, it's almost a physical strike. What I thought was a table is actually an altar. Here on top of this mountain is a site of offering. We've scaled the rocky cliff to find a sacred place at the top. This is totally unexpected, and my spirit is stirred. My thoughts are racing. What am I seeing here? An altar... I know my eyes are bugging out now because I'm so surprised by this discovery.

The Sacrifice

Something is on the altar and at first, I'm stunned again. I see flesh. Oh my. I'm certain it's a sacrifice. Ever so closely, I examine the object on the altar. Yes, it's a sacrifice. But it isn't burning, and I know from studying the Word that that's not good. I almost panic. Why isn't it burning? I look up at the sky.

"Lord, why isn't this sacrifice burning? Isn't it meant to burn? Oh, I know the answer to that. I remember Your word and the sacrifices in the Bible stories. God, You're supposed to send fire to burn and consume it. Unless . . ."

Panic is really setting in now and I scramble to try to figure this out. Immediately I realize how the people in ancient Bible times must've felt, waiting for their sacrifices to be accepted by God. It almost makes me want to hold my breath, nearly in a panic.

"Lord, please accept this sacrifice."

But it just lays there. Unaffected. Cold. My heart is racing because I know the sacrifice absolutely must be acceptable. It simply must be.

"Oh Lord, what do we do?" My mind races, quickly trying to find the reason it's not burning. "What are You saying, Lord? This sacrifice: what does it mean?" I look to the Word. "Lead me, Lord. Tell me."

The Sacrifice of Praise

Scripture says, "Bring the sacrifice of praise into the house of the Lord."

". . . Bringing sacrifices of praise to the house of the Lord." Jeremiah 17:26

"Therefore, by Him let us continually offer the sacrifice of praise to God, that is, the fruit of our lips, giving thanks to His name." Hebrews 13:15 NKJV

"Lord, is this about praise?"

I run to look in my Bible to read about the 'evening sacrifice', because it looks like evening here on the mountain with the glow of the sunset through the trees. *Ps 141: 2 says 'Let my prayer be set before you as incense; and the lifting up of my hands as the evening sacrifice'. (NKJV)* Exodus 29 teaches us that it is a continual offering. Every evening. Every evening, every praise. I see the fleshly thing on that altar, and now I believe this is my word from the Lord to get our praise in line. I swallow hard and begin to pray.

Not Just Our Own Ability

Now, I lead our worship team on Sundays. It's clear to me that I must apply this lesson to us first and then share it with others so they can also learn. Reflecting on the most recent service, I know that what we offered was fleshly. We were struggling, making efforts in our own abilities, and we must do all we can to change that. We can't lean on our own abilities to do anything. It must be by Him and through Him. He must be allowed to pour worship through us. We are nothing without Him.

"Lord, we'll change this. We *will* change this." I must seek out the answer in Him. "How do we do this, Lord? Tell me and we'll follow. I'm determined to change whatever we need to change."

The Towel

Then I remember the towel Jesus had on His arm before we began our journey up the mountainside. I'd almost forgotten about it. I ask Him because I don't want to just leave it there. I know it's important because Jesus brought it with Him; it must mean something. He brings my thoughts to the scripture in John chapter 13 about the time when He used a towel to teach 'serving one another' to His disciples at the Last Supper. In the ultimate display of serving and loving, Jesus had wrapped a towel around Himself like a servant would and knelt to wash each disciple's feet.

Reflection and Revelation

This vision was a total surprise for me. I've tried to convey it as best as I can: the climb, the astonishment of seeing the altar and the fleshly offering. As I look back on the memory of this time with Jesus, I can almost smell that rock cliff, feel the hardness of the cold, flinty stone. It was an experience of deep discussion with the Lord.

The towel teaches servanthood. 'By love, serve one another' must be a key. Jesus had a team: His disciples. And He taught them to serve one another. That theme is also how I teach my worship team. Oh my, Jesus, how I needed this. How much I needed this. If we're serving, then we're looking outside of ourselves. We can't focus on ourselves and serve at the same time.

I love Him so much for taking the time to instruct me. How awesome it is that our Lord, the King of the universe and beyond, takes the time for us individually. Wow, what amazing love! He took the time to show me where we can grow. Oh, how I love Him! I'm totally transparent with this one, hoping that some may learn by the instruction of the Lord to me. He teaches us so we can grow.

Moving Into Other Dimensions – Veils, Gates, Portals, Doorways

Galatians 5:25
NKJV

If we live in the Spirit,
Let us also walk in the Spirit.

~ Journal Entry Day 10 ~

Prayer Time ~

EACH DAY NOW, I begin my quiet time with the Lord's Prayer. The Holy Spirit is unfolding it, revealing so much depth and beauty as I make it my personal plea. And then I wait for Him.

In a vision, Jesus stands before me, and behind Him is a beautiful meadow, laid out in brilliant colors. He's pouring crystal clear liquid from a gleaming silver jar with a gold band around the top. The vessel He's pouring into appears to be made of a leather hide of some kind, and is tied at the top with a leather type cord.

"You'll need this," He tells me, as He loads it onto Abraham just behind his head. Then the Lord smiles at me, "Ready to go?"

I mount up. What? I'm amazed at myself. I just climbed up on my horse with ease, completely mounted.

"Hey!" I call out.

I'm so happy to have accomplished this feat that I can't help but let Jesus know. My Savior looks and kind of chuckles and nods. I think He's proud of me for mounting Abraham on my own; I sure am. This is a first for me.

The Covenant Reminder

All at once, a rainbow appears and surrounds me. Actually, it swirls around and envelopes me. The warm rainbow almost feels like an embrace, and I'm completely covered. There's a welcoming, loving feeling to it. I know that sounds impossible, but it's the only way I know to describe the experience.

"The rainbow reminds me of Your precious covenant, Lord, Your holy agreement." The word 'covenant' has such a sweet sound to me.

Jesus says, "My covenant, a contract sealed by the rainbow, is a promise of My love. With it, I have made an oath never to flood the earth again."

"Lord, I always love Your rainbows. They make me think of You. Whenever I see one, I want to stay and watch until it just disappears."

He allows me to remain in the prisms of color as they swirl around me. I feel I could stay here forever, basking in this atmosphere. It's a love that surrounds me, this oath from our covenant God! I have a guarantee from our promise-keeping Lord, and He assures me of His everlasting pledge. He's in this for us, forever. Just *wow*!

Then I hear Him say, "Abraham, let's go."

Another Dimension

We begin at a faster pace this time, trotting alongside a bright, crystal white sea. I can see Jesus ahead of me and the wind is blowing His hair back. That precious Wind. After a while, He comes to a stop and dismounts. Then He and the horses gaze across the glistening body of water. We're all looking toward an entrance into another dimension. That's the only way I know how to describe the opening in the sky. We draw near and slowly move into the other world.

On the other side of the entrance is a world of blue sky and clouds. There's nothing under our feet except the heavens, with a stunning blue sky and brilliant white clouds. We approach a stairway which is glistening with a crystal-like golden color. A horse comes near. Another horse! This one is solid white. Jesus strokes its head with a gentle greeting.

Heaven's Castles

The long golden stair climbs an extremely high mountain with a throne on the very top. I can't see the entirety of this throne because the atmosphere is incredibly bright, and the throne is immense. This is the very centerpiece of this entire place. Everything seems to lead to it and from it. Jesus shows me castles and settlements all around the path and the mountainsides. The gigantic height is almost too big to call it a mountain. There are so very many incredibly huge golden castles all over it. People walk up and down the pathway to the throne. They are experiencing such a peace, such a tremendous peace. I've never seen anything like it. There are so many of these fortresses, all massive in size and incredible in beauty. I feel I'm gazing on a vast Kingdom of kingdoms.

Jesus looks at me. "You need to see this place, not just the entrance to hell."

"Tell them to never fear death. Those that I hold never fear death. You see the heaven I have prepared for those who accept Me as their Savior."

All of this is beyond words. Who wouldn't want to come here?

"Lord, You've created this magnificent place and I'm so anxious to tell everyone how wonderful it is."

Abraham comes up beside me and I mount up again. Haha! I did it! Jesus smiles again. Have I said how much I love that smile? Oh sweet, sweet Savior.

The Water of the Word

As we're traveling, the white horse that Jesus caressed approaches and nuzzles next to Abraham. These two know each other. I'm sure that at some point I'll learn this white beauty's name, but evidently not today. I'm content with that.

"Whatever You want Lord, is what I want."

Once again, we near the entrance of the veils. Jesus tells me about the vessel of water that He filled and placed on my horse's neck.

"This one's for Abraham."

Well, I'm a bit astounded. My mind is racing with thoughts. This is for Abraham? Isn't he a heavenly creature? What does this mean? He needs water? Abraham needs water? I know I look astounded again. Jesus is so patient with me and my questions.

"This is the water of the Word. I Am the Word. (Oh my... He pours it.) Abraham needs this too. All are upheld by My Word. Everything exists by My Word." Then He strokes Abraham's mane and says, "Isn't that right, ole boy" in such tender and loving tones.

This... oh my... *this* truth. My understanding is being opened again. Abraham, my walk of faith, is nurtured and upheld by the Word. *His* word. I look at this gorgeous creature. 'Oh, I will nurture you. I will definitely keep this vessel filled for you,' I promise in my heart. My precious Bible is even more dear to me now than ever. I'll fill up on His precious Word. Time *in* the Word and time *with* the Word...

A Test for Me

Jesus is behind us now, walking in a different direction than we are. I look back at Him, not sure why He's not beside us. Abraham stands facing the original path, and again, I'm full of questions. What am I to do at this point? It's decision time and I feel it. My horse stands ready to go. If I move forward, Abraham will too, but should I? Is this what's known as a step of faith? Is the Lord sending me out? Is that what I'm supposed to do? I can't help but look at Jesus walking the other way. Do we turn around?

At that moment, something enormous arises in me and I declare loudly with a great deal of boldness, "I won't take a single step without You, Jesus! I will *not* go forward without You in front leading the way!"

The Lord stops and turns around, and roars out a laugh. Yes, *roars* out a laugh. I wasn't expecting this at all. I'm stunned. He comes back, mounts His horse, takes the reins and we start a heavenly ride. He's out in front of me (& Abraham) and is absolutely glorious, riding through heavenly blue sky full of gorgeous, shimmering white and bright yellow clouds. The Maker of the universe is magnificent, and His voice booms. I can't say it big enough. Jesus is convulsing with glee, and it rumbles all through the heavenlies. I mean it's a resounding, joyous reverberation. His voice is enormous. I'm so amazed I can hardly breathe. This vibrant, ringing laugh feels like a proclamation coming out of Him! He's making a declaration.

"Not without Me; did you hear that?" He's bellowing with joy. It *is* a declaration. And He's joyfully ringing it out through the heavens.

Reflection and Revelation

I consider the vessel of water. Our walk of faith is fed and strengthened by the Word of Almighty God. We must daily seek out that treasure, the satisfying water of His Word. Jesus is the only way of salvation. I find it so amazing that the jar Jesus held was pure silver and gold and that He poured this water into a simple leather bag. It's such a beautiful picture of the way He pours heavenly treasure into us, mere human containers. God is so good to us. So, so good. Isn't it exciting to know He's prepared a Kingdom of kingdoms for us? I don't know all that we'll be doing in that heavenly realm, but just this small glimpse of what He has prepared for us lets me know that we'll be busy and loving every minute of it. How could we not love everything about Him?

The last little part I know must've been a test for me. I'm compelled to follow Jesus no matter what, never taking off on my own accord. Not without Jesus; never without my Jesus. My, oh my! I can't describe the feeling of astounding joy that flew though me when He roared out that laugh. But it also solidified something in me, hammering it down deep in my soul.

Extra insight is given today. The Holy Spirit opens my understanding about the canisters left at the veil entrance. Each container represents a chapter, and the corded tie joins them together in a book about my experiences with the Lord in the heavenlies.

***Luke 15:7*
*NKJV***

*"I say to you that likewise
there will be more joy in heaven over one sinner who repents,
than over ninety-nine just persons
who need no repentance."*

~ Journal Entry Day 11 ~

—The Lamb's Book of Life —

Today, Lord, what would You like to say to me? I'm here, anxious to hear Your voice. I long for Your presence and I wait.

Abraham is Decked Out

Each time I see Abraham, I'm amazed at his attractiveness. In addition to his shimmering gold mane and tail, I see he's also been given a sparkling gold blanket, spread across his back. He's decked out with jewels: emeralds, diamonds, sapphires and rubies in his mane and tail.

"Lord, what is this?" I ask as I am gazing at Abraham.

Jesus answers my question. "He is getting ready for the big day."

To our right is a long path leading to a faraway place that is brilliantly gold and bright. I can see bright outlines of the structures there. A person surely needs to be properly adorned for an entrance into that glorious realm. You can't just walk in there any ole' which way, no siree. It demands a certain protocol. Elegance. Beauty. Holiness.

There is No Answer

I look to Jesus and His brow is curled a bit with a questioning look. "Why don't they want to come? Why don't they want to come here?"

I know what He's asking. Why don't people want to come to heaven, where He is? I'm at a loss, trying to think through the reasons. All the possible answers go through my head, but they seem so small in comparison to the sight before me. The flimsy reasons for not loving Jesus have no weight at all. I can't even bring myself to speak out all the reasons people have given me over the years. I cannot say them aloud, not while standing in this magnificent place. Every excuse I've ever heard seems so frivolous in His presence.

"Oh, my Lord, only You know the hearts of men. Only You . . ."

My heart aches for Him. I know He really knows the answer, but He's allowing me to see with Him. Oh, my heart! I want everyone to see and know Him, to behold Him in His beauty and His awesome love.

The Precious Pages

My Savior looks upward and stretches His hand to point. I look where He's indicating, and then He takes my hand. We ascend, higher and higher. There's an opening before us, very similar to the opening in the heavens that I've seen before with Him. In mere moments, we are on the other side of the entrance in a massive, open cosmic place. Stars and galaxies are scattered all around us. The Lord is no longer beside me, but out in front facing me, and He encompasses this entire place. The Supreme Almighty is right in front of me. The cosmos can't contain Him. I don't think we realize just how immense... vast... enormous... He is. Our God is THE AWESOME MAGNIFICENT GOD!

Then I see Him holding a large, open book. He's gazing at it, lovingly caressing the pages. I realize by the way He's looking at the massive volume that it's the Lamb's Book of Life [6], and it's extremely special to Him. His hand gently skims over the precious pages.

The Plea

I'm able to see lines of writing on the pages, and He puts His hand on them.

In an agonizing voice He says, "One day, the last name will be written." Tears start rolling down my cheeks. So much louder, and with so much passion that my heart is about to burst, Jesus declares, "One day, THE LAST NAME will be written."

His face. His voice. The sound of it echoes throughout endless space. I want someone to hear it and respond to His pleading. He's imploring, beseeching, begging. Oh, how I want people to respond to His insistence. Can't you hear it? Oh, please, can't you hear His sweet voice calling you? Oh, my heart. I sob violently for quite some time, just weeping before Him. I'm crying out for those I know who are lost without Him right now.

Heavenly Rewards

Next, I see names come flying through the cosmos to land on the pages of Jesus's book. There's an immediate response in the heavenly Kingdom just beyond us. I hear rejoicing, laughter, and cheering. The letters forming the names of people on earth are not exactly on a screen, but they appear like a hologram of sorts suspended in midair. All the people living in heaven are so happy, celebrating at the sight of every single name that appears. An immediate uproar explodes as familiar names join the pages. The people who recognize family members and friends break out into a party, rejoicing with great celebration.

There are others receiving a reward as each person's name is recorded. The name is suspended in midair just before coming to rest on the page, and a sparkle of light flies off it to land on a certain person. The sparkle adorns them. As I watch this happen over and over, I come to understand that these individuals helped those people find their way to Christ. Perhaps they had spoken a word, shown them love, given them a Bible... all acts which are like planting seeds that grow into a decision. Now they're receiving a special reward as the newborn Christians' names appear. Sparks of light. Beautiful!

Reflection and Revelation

Lord, let us never forget that we hold a dear treasure that needs to be shared with everyone: the awesome message of salvation. Seeing this vision made me realize just how much it means when we lead someone to salvation in Christ. It has an eternal impact, of course. The birthing of that precious soul into the Kingdom of our dear Savior rings out in the heavens and everyone there celebrates. We must introduce people to Jesus. We simply must.

Traveling Instructions

Matthew 6:9-13
KJV

9 After this manner therefore pray ye: Our Father which art in heaven,

Hallowed be Thy name.

10 Thy Kingdom come. Thy will be done in earth, as it is in heaven.

11 Give us this day our daily bread.

12 And forgive us our debts, as we forgive our debtors.

13 And lead us not into temptation, but deliver us from evil: For Thine is the Kingdom, and the power, and the glory, forever. Amen.

1 Peter 5:7
NKJV

Casting all your care upon Him,
for He cares for you.

~ Journal Entry Day 12 ~

— Keep Your Load Light —

Each day now, I begin my quiet time with the Lord's Prayer. The Holy Spirit is unfolding it, revealing so much depth and beauty as I make it my personal plea.

My Father – You are my Creator, Sustainer, and Keeper, the Source of my beginning.

Who art in Heaven–Heavenly Father, You're not from this earth. I have an earthly Dad given to me by You, my Father in Heaven, which is my real homeland, my true abode.

Hallowed be Thy name – Your name, oh God, is holy and righteous, and there's no other name equal to Your great name. You have all the power and deserve all the glory.

Your Kingdom come and Your will be done on earth as it is in Heaven – Your Kingdom; not mine, but Yours. Your Kingdom is what I long for. Oh my Father, I want Your will to be done here on earth just like it is in heaven. How I love Your Kingdom.

Give me this day my daily bread – Lord, I can't survive without you. Meet with me daily to talk and be close. Your presence is my bread. Your sacrifice sustains me and will carry me to my homeland. You provide all my needs and give me even more so I can be a blessing to others. Oh, thank You so much.

And forgive me my trespasses as I forgive those who trespass against me – I give You every hurt now, and choose to forgive anyone who has abused, hurt, distressed, harmed, taken advantage of or wrongly used me. It's my choice not to hold any offense in my heart. With Your help, I release them and forgive them. Please forgive me for all my failures and shortcomings, and any wrongs I have willingly or innocently done to others.

Lead me not into temptation, but deliver me from evil – Thank You, Lord, that You've made a way for me to choose not to give in to temptation. You lead me in a plain path. Deliver me from the evil and darkness in this world. You're my Light.

For Yours is the Kingdom and the Power and the Glory forever – The Kingdom of Heaven belongs to You. Everything in my life is Yours, and I'll give You all the honor and glory and praise as long as I live.

And I wait before Him. Where Is He?

Abraham greets me, his glistening mane and tail so captivating. I take a moment to admire his magnificent beauty and stroke him, then climb up on his back to wait for Jesus. The place we're standing in is so stunning. We're on a path, looking over a landscape of gently rolling mountains that are absolutely alive with color. All around us are gloriously hued flowers and trees of deepest green.

I don't see Jesus yet. So, I ask, "Where is He Abraham? I know He's here." There's an urge to search Him out, so we move along the pathway. Ahead is a bit of a clearing with flowery vines hanging from a few of the trees on the rim. So beautiful.

"Abraham," I cry out. "Do you smell that fragrance? It's Him. I know it's Him!"

I dismount and am immediately drawn to a small lake up ahead. Nearing the shoreline, I kneel and put my hand in the water. Just as I do, I see Jesus's hand reaching into it too.

"Oh Jesus, You're here! I'm so happy, so overjoyed!"

Casting Our Care Upon Him

We move away from the lake together and mount the horses. After traveling for a bit along this path, I sense something moving nearby. Jesus stops and gets down, and I do as He does. He lets the horses go just a step or two ahead, leaving us on foot. I notice I'm wearing sandals this time.

Suddenly someone is pushing boxes and crates toward me. The containers are tied with ropes and appear to be moving boxes and trunks. It looks to me like someone has loaded up everything in their house; loads and loads of stuff. The people are trying to get on the path with us, but they need help with all the moving boxes. All at once I find myself buried in the pile of large, loaded crates, and can't move. I certainly can't lift it all.

"Lord, what am I supposed to do with this? I can't carry these for them, but they want to go down the path and evidently need help. What do I do?"

"These boxes are not yours to carry. The people need to give them to Me; even the largest trunks are small to Me."

I remember seeing His hand when He held the sun in it. Oh, these containers truly are nothing to Him.

"Encourage the people to give their burdens to Me because you can't carry them. The boxes are a heavy weight to you and will hinder you on your own journey. Love the people enough to get them to look to Me for help. If you try to do it, you'll hurt yourself *and them* in the process. Push the people toward Me; I'll take their load."

It's true: I can't take on someone else's burdens. I simply must show them the way to Jesus, the only one who can truly help them with the heavy things they carry. I must introduce them to the real Answer, Jesus.

Don't Get Entangled

After this lesson, we walk a bit further and I feel something around my ankle. I look down and discover there's a vine trying to wrap itself around my foot. What? I'm irritated by this scraggly thing trying to hold on to me. I struggle free from it and lean closer into Jesus.

"What is that thing? What's it doing?"

"It's the cares of life that will tangle you up and keep you from your path."

His response causes me to think of cares that weigh me down.

"Lingering too long," He says.

Now I understand. Spending too much time holding on to the cares of life gives this creepy vine a chance to totally wrap itself around me. The care and worry of it, the sleepless nights. Oh my. There's no need for me to allow myself to become anxious when I can just totally give it all to Jesus. Lingering too long on the challenges and troubles I face causes me to stop and get bogged down with the worry. The cares of life can keep me from spending time in His presence. Worry will stifle me.

"Lord, I must not be entangled in the affairs of earthly life. I must live life, of course, and take care of my responsibilities here, but the cares of this life are not for me. I'll give You all the burdens and weights of my life. You're the One who cares for me. I need to trust you completely; that's the faith walk. The sparrows do not plant or toil, but You feed them. And You care for us even more. The lilies of the field are beautifully adorned, but they're not working to spin their colorful clothes. You provide their beauty.[7] Help me to remember this precious part of Your word, Lord. Thank You, thank You, thank You, thank You!"

Jesus looks at me and says, "Let's ride now. Just ride."

"Yes Lord! Always."

Reflection and Revelation

Too many times, we're slowed down on our path by the cares of this life. Isn't that what Martha faced? (Luke 10) She was 'cumbered about' with the serving. Was serving bad? No, it was necessary. But her heart had become weighted with the care of it and that affected her attitude toward her sister, Mary.

When we find ourselves becoming laden down with a worry or concern, we must immediately run to Jesus with it. We don't want to hold onto it until it wraps its creepy little fingers around us. Too much weight to carry can stall us on our journey.

"Lord, please help us to release the burdens and worries of this life to You. Show us how to serve with a light heart that has totally given the care of everything to You."

Note of caution: to release the care doesn't mean we take on an attitude of 'I don't care'. No; we are to love deeply. To release the care is simply to put our whole trust in Jesus rather than carrying the worry and fretting over things.

"Jesus, help me to remember this lesson You've beautifully shown me today. I can love and even help my loved ones, but I can't carry any load that's supposed to be given to You. We must encourage one another to come to You, the only One Who can lift the load from our hearts. I can't reach the heart of a person, but You can." How beautifully the Psalmist says it, *"But You, Lord are a shield around me, my glory, and the One Who Lifts My Head." Psalm 3:3*

Psalm 32:8
NKJV

I will instruct you and teach you in the way you should go;
I will guide you with my eye.

~ Journal Entry Day 13 ~

—Viewpoint of Heaven—

I'M EAGER TO be in God's presence today. Everything else seems so blah and boring. Nothing compares to His companionship. No program, movie, activity, or amusement equals being with the King of kings. I find myself hurrying to finish my work to spend time with Him. I worship Him, pray, and sing, and then I wait.

God's Paradigm, Not Man's

There's Jesus's smiling face. Oh, that expression is like a refreshing drink for my soul. It's life to me. Everything fades in comparison. All worries seem to vanish. His presence is total peace.

We're looking out from what appears to be the bow of a ship. It's fashioned like a tall ship or schooner with tremendous sails, a wooden ship's wheel and huge ropes coiled on the deck. The vast sea sparkles everywhere the sun hits the waves, various shades of blue in constant motion. I notice that I have a telescope in my hand, which I examine and then lift up to look through. Jesus takes it for a moment, looks at it briefly, and tosses it out across the sea.

As it spins away, He explains, "You need to see through My eyes. This telescope is Man's design. When you use it, you're seeing everything through human perspective. I am your eyes."

'Oh wow,' I think. "Yes, Lord." I'm quick to embrace His instruction.

I scan the sky, and we look out across the sea for a few moments.

"Do you like traveling with Abraham better, or sailing on the ship?" Jesus asks abruptly.

I can't help myself and laugh a little. He does too.

"Anywhere *You* are, Lord. Anywhere You are."

We walk around on the deck of the ship. These ropes are huge!

"I navigate the waters. My vision is so much more than the mere devices of men. I see what man's vision can't possibly see: the depths of the waters, the obstacles under the surface for this ship to avoid. I'll adjust the sails to change speed or direction to ensure a safe landing on shore, taking you to the place where I need you to be. You don't want to crash before you even begin."

The lesson amazes me again.

Reflection and Revelation

The ship represents more than a pleasurable trip. It's the picture of our life. We need to learn to depend on God's wisdom to guide us in our life, rather than relying on Man. The Lord speeds us up or slows us down according to what is needed. We must trust that He loves us enough to keep us from shipwreck if we just listen. Isn't it amazing that He will even slow us down to keep us from crashing? He loves us so. Sometimes we know where we're headed, but miss the timing. If we move forward on our own, or ignore His leading, it can mean a headlong crash onto a 'shoreline' we were meant to reach safely. Impatience can run our ship aground.

"Lord, help me follow Your guidance as You change direction and timing in my life. You're ordering my steps. Please help me not to crash before I even begin."

Genesis 2:7
KJV

7 And the Lord God formed man of the dust of the ground, and breathed into his nostrils the breath of life; and man became a living soul.

~ Journal Entry Day 14 ~

—By Him, For Him, From Him —

MY TIME BEGINS with worship, then I wait patiently before the Lord.

I see an object that looks like a big shovel, scooping something that rolls up like ice cream being dipped. The substance is a light gold color with golden sparkles and glittering jewels on the crust. Jesus is in profile, and stoops down to gather the unusual material. It looks so creamy, and I think maybe it would taste good, but that seems crazy because it's coming from the ground. It's very appealing.

Together, Jesus and I scoop it up and load it in a wagon. We proceed to haul our load down a pathway that crosses a very high cliff on the side of a mountain. This trail overlooks a gorgeous green valley with a crystal water stream deep below. I'm amazed that I'm perfectly at ease, not giving a thought to the height. I look to Jesus.

"What's this stuff from the ground that we're carrying?"

"It's from the foundation of heaven." He answered.

Okay, that makes sense; we scooped it up from the ground there. I realize the substance is going to be poured. But on what or where? My mind races: is it going to be poured out on a person or a place or what? Jesus reminds me of the mold from many days before this. He's going to pour this substance into that shaped container. I'm aware that I'm big-eyed because that's the weapon I saw in the cottage . . .

The Lord clarifies it for me. "I've formed Man from the dust of the earth. But I form him in the Spirit realm as well, from the dust, the very foundation of heaven. He is spirit formed of Spirit."

My mind is filled with the thought of our creation. We were formed by Him, constructed of the ground of heaven and earth. Jesus, You are the foundation of all things, including heaven and earth. This golden material is You, Your very essence. The thought is so much more than I can possibly absorb at the moment.

"Lord, I'm overwhelmed. How do I grasp this?" My mind is trying so hard to embrace the concept. There are gold and jewels in the foundation of heaven, and we are formed by Him with particles of heaven; from Him. I only know that I feel so loved and treasured. I'm the daughter of a great and marvelous King. He carefully molds us so magnificently. Wow... my heart is so full.

Reflection and Revelation

From the heavens we were formed. We are His idea. The creamy golden substance and the jewels in it lets me know how precious we are in His sight. We're His creation, His beautiful, wonderfully made treasure. Created by Him, for Him, and from Him. We are His, made from Him. The wonder moves my heart to love Him even more. We came from Him, and we'll return to Him. I can hardly wait! We long for Your return, Lord.

Assignments

Isaiah 62:6-7
NKJV

6 I have set watchmen on your walls, O Jerusalem; They shall never hold their peace day or night. You who make mention of the Lord, do not keep silent,

7 And give Him no rest till He establishes and till He makes Jerusalem a praise in the earth.

Jeremiah 29:7
NKJV

7 And seek the peace of the city where I have caused you to be carried away captive, and pray to the Lord for it: for in its peace, you will have peace.

~ Journal Entry Day 15 ~

—Assignments —

I WORSHIP AND sing today. The song I'm listening to urges me to dance, so here in my quiet space, I move in worship before Him. Oh, in the real world, I'm no dancer; I have two left feet. Ha ha. But here in His presence, it's very different. I pray and then I wait.

Called Into the Place of Intercession

Jesus's expression is very intent. That's the only way I can think of to describe it. Dressed in His Kingly attire, His crown and robe, He mounts His horse. There's a very weighty atmosphere today. He's riding out front. I don't speak a lot because the King is on a mission, a moment that demands a magnitude of reverence. We're on a steep mountain, walking a narrow path cut into the side. The massive height is very high, and the trail overlooks a deep valley or gorge. I trust. I'm not afraid, because He's with me.

Abraham is so sure-footed. He's actually moving in a bit of a prance. I chuckle at him because it's as if he wants me to know that he's sure about his ability to walk this narrow road. What a creature!

We walk for quite a piece, climbing the steep path, then reach a point where the horses can go no further. Dismounting, we climb the last little stretch of the way on foot. It's not too far, and Jesus reaches a hand back to pull me up at the end. At last, we've reached the top of this extremely high peak. It's so high, it seems as if we can see the entire world from here. Jesus gazes over the vast expanse. He's so regal and majestic in His Kingly attire. I have a strong sense that He's going to "declare a thing."[18] He looks over at me, then turns back toward the landscape below.

"I'm about to roar," He proclaims, "and the whole earth will hear it. Some may not believe, but those who believe will hear and understand. They'll see. The roar will cover the earth."

I see America and begin to cry for my nation. I can't help myself; the tears pour out of me. I cry out for my country with a powerful burden. There are so many challenges facing us now.

"My Kingdom is so much bigger." With a wave of His hand, I can see the greatness of His Kingdom.

But America is on my heart, and I begin to intercede and weep for her.

Tenderly, the Lord tells me, "I see what burdens you, and even what you haven't yet seen. I *will* move. I've heard the prayers, the heart cries from My Church, and I will answer."

Jesus mounts His horse and pulls me up to ride with Him. Oh my... *with* Him... what is this? I'm overwhelmed, but I simply obey.

"Whatever You want Lord, I obey."

He's still in His Kingly attire, and we ride. I become aware that He's taking me all over the United States, one state at a time. We're riding above my country, which looks like a map below us. He waits for me to intercede and declare His name and His word over each one. Individual states kind of pop up from the map below us. Next, we ride over all the rest of the earth and Jesus waits for me to declare His word over every country. I call out the name of each one as it comes into view and proclaim that Jesus is Lord over the whole earth.

"Come! Come! Come!" Jesus declares, and I proclaim what He does. We linger over the Middle East, and the call is "Come! Come! Come!"

When we are finished, we soak in the atmosphere of victory before we dismount.

Thy Kingdom Come

"I've put My roar in My Church. They must roar, declare, and decree My word over the earth. Declare 'Thy Kingdom Come! Thy Kingdom Come!'"

I can almost see Jesus as the Lion of Judah when He opens His mouth to roar. I see the Church as she opens her mouth to roar His proclamation. We can't just sit idle; we must declare and decree, 'Thy Kingdom come, Lord. Thy Kingdom come!'

Reflection and Revelation

Do we truly understand that our nation needs us to pray and intercede for her? We must declare Jesus's word over our struggling country. Intercession in our regular prayer time is essential, but at times we need to go further, to pray more deeply, to travail in prayer. That's when we follow His voice and share His agony over people, places, nations, and circumstances. We 'ride' with Him and say what He says. Sweet intercessor, precious prayer warrior, cry out with our Lord. Let your voice ring out with His. The Spirit of the Lord will give you the urgency.

2 Chronicles 7:14
KJV

*¹⁴ If my people, which are called by my name,
shall humble themselves, and pray, and seek my face,
and turn from their wicked ways;
then will I hear from heaven,
and will forgive their sin, and will heal their land.*

~ Journal Entry Day 16 ~

—Assignment to Intercession —

"Lord, all earthly things are fading into momentary obscurity. Your Word, Your presence are my daily sustenance. How wonderful You are."

I pray, I worship and . . . I wait.

Flood Of His Glory

Jesus and I are standing side by side, looking into an opening that leads into another place, a different dimension. There's a solid stone gate constructed of big rocks; it looks like a castle wall. This huge gate holds back a golden, sparkling clear body of water that's alive with sunlight, glowing with fiery yellows. I can tell the lake is almost ready to burst through the gate. Just beyond is a beautiful mountain. The bright sun is pouring over it, spilling down onto the water. I realize I'm seeing a flood, but it's so beautiful, bright, and gold that it must be a good flood. It occurs to me that it's the outpouring of God's glory that we so desperately need.

"Lord, please open it! Open the flood gate and let Your glory pour over our land."

I become aware that the sides of the huge gate are held in place by large 'pins' of some kind. They slide down into iron brackets like huge hinges. Angels are holding and watching over the pins.

"Lord, what are those connectors? Do they hold back the flood of Your glory, the awakening for our nation?"

I know that when those pins are removed, the gate will fall open and the flood will be released.

Turn

When I look closer, I notice that there's writing on the heads of the pins, which simply reads *'Turn.'* I think, 'Okay, they must twist like screws.' But then Jesus reminds me of the scripture we all quote now: *"If My people who are called by My name will humble themselves and pray and seek My face and <u>turn</u> from their wicked ways, <u>then</u> I will hear from heaven and will forgive their sin and heal their land." 2 Chronicles 7:14 KJV*

TURN! That's it: *turn* from their wicked ways. Then He will hear. As we turn, these pins turn to release His glory.

"Lord, what are our wicked ways?"

Talking it over with Jesus gives me an inner knowing of the answer. We're so influenced by evil that our understanding of exactly what evil is has been perverted by the culture. Few people look at the true Word of God and receive it 'as is', let alone accept it as a guideline.

"Oh Lord, please help us to turn!"

Reflection and Revelation

As I reflect on this precious vision, I'm certain that the glory awaits us if we just turn! The glory of God is available. We must preach the turning, teach it, and live it. Let's cooperate as a partner with God to release His glory.

I ponder the term 'wicked ways' and consider the Ten Commandments as a starting point.

Exodus 20:2-17 NKJV

2 You shall have <u>no other gods before Me.</u>

3 <u>You shall not make for yourself a carved image</u> – any likeness of anything that is in heaven above, or that is in the earth beneath, or that is in the water under the earth,

5 You shall not bow down to them nor serve them. For I, the Lord your God, am a jealous God, visiting the iniquity of the fathers upon the children to the third and fourth generations of those who hate Me,

6 but showing mercy to thousands, to those who love Me and keep My commandments.

7 <u>You shall not take the name of the Lord you God in vain</u>, for the Lord will not hold him guiltless who takes His name in vain.

8 <u>Remember the Sabbath day, to keep it holy</u>.

9 Six days you shall labor and do all your work,

10 but the seventh day is the Sabbath of the Lord your God. In it you shall do no work: you nor your son, nor your daughter, nor your male servant, nor your female servant, nor your cattle, nor your stranger who is within your gates.

11 For in six days the Lord make the heavens and the earth, the sea, and all that is in them, and rested the seventh day. Therefore the Lord blessed the Sabbath day and hallowed it.

12 <u>Honor your father and your mother</u>, that your days may be long upon the land which the Lord your God is giving you.

13 <u>You shall not murder</u>.

14 <u>You shall not commit adultery</u>.

15 <u>You shall not steal</u>.

16 <u>You shall not bear false witness</u> against your neighbor.

17 <u>You shall not covet</u> your neighbor's house; you shall not covet your neighbor's wife, nor his male servant, nor his female servant, nor his ox, nor his donkey, nor anything that is your neighbor's.

<u>No gods before Me</u>. None. Yet we have so many things that stand in our way of worship. What things stand in front of God? What comes first in our daily lives?

<u>Don't take His name in vain</u>. Yet on every television show, in every public place, even from the lips of children now, we hear the wrongful use of His beautiful name. Are we aware how often we use it disrespectfully?

<u>Remember the Sabbath</u>. Unless you want to do something else. Anything else. Think: do we remember, or do we forget? Has it become just another day of pursuing OUR own interests?

<u>Don't kill</u>. But wait, it isn't killing; it's called "choice." Do we turn from conflict and say it's none of our business? Help us, Lord.

<u>Don't commit adultery</u>. The excuses run like a river. Is it really acceptable to think, 'everybody does it'?

And the list goes on and on. How far we have slipped from the pure Word! Our vision isn't clear; we need the Holy Spirit to purify it. My heart is broken.

"Oh, Lord, bring us back. Bring us back to the pure Word."

We must turn from wicked ways! As I study to identify what God considers wicked, I know we must turn away from them, avoid them. When we know His Word, we must choose to run from the things He identifies as wicked. When we do, the pins will begin to turn, the gate will open, and we will experience that flood of the glory of God.

"God, please help us to turn. Help me do my part."

Little Confirmations

Amazing little confirmations are such sweet touches from our Lord. With the most incredible timing He gives me experiences that verify the meanings of my visions. When I had the vision of the rainbow around me, I wrote in my journal about what the Lord had shown me. Then my daughter and I went to the beach; we were nearly 300 miles from home. That very day, my social media newsfeed was blowing up with a multitude of pictures that people were taking of rainbows appearing *in the area of our home – my community!* Later, I saw a posting from someone who was creating a pretty wall hanging with jewels and a gold horseshoe. A gold horseshoe!

"Thank you, Lord, for these little nudges that let me know You are really here. You really are. Oh, how I love You."

John 10:27
KJV

*My sheep hear My voice
and I know them and they follow Me*

~ Journal Entry Day 17 ~

—His Voice—

I'VE STARTED TO pray at the closing of my day as well as first thing in the morning. Tonight, I can't help but look for Him, and I simply ask, "Lord, is there anything You want to say to me?" Then I wait in His presence.

I spot Jesus just ahead of me, looking out across a crystal blue sea. The water is shimmering with lights, like sparkling diamonds. He steps out into the ocean and of course I follow. We're not walking *on* the water. Nope. We're letting the water just roll up on us. When we reach the right depth, we start to swim, and the water is dancing around us. Wow: there's no other way to describe the way the sea is moving.

"Immerse yourself in My love."

Swim around in that sweet Spirit? Absolutely! I'm totally undone. There are no words for this experience. Nothing compares with the love Jesus has for us. Nothing.

When it's time to leave and walk back out of the crystal water, I discover that we're not dripping wet. Now that is something! We mount up on our horses and travel.

The Darkness

The path we're riding on becomes narrow and suddenly everything is black. Dense black. I've lost sight of Jesus in front of me; I see nothing but darkness. What happened? His presence was so real just moments ago. What is this? I know Abraham is still with me because I'm riding him. Whew! What a relief that I haven't lost him. This darkness has engulfed me, and I hold on to Abraham tightly.

"Jesus!" I call out. "JESUS!"

"Hold on to Abraham and follow My voice. Just follow My voice." His voice is so reassuring.

I really don't like this darkness, but if I have His voice, I'm not afraid. As long as I know my horse is here too, I'll be okay. The powerful stallion doesn't seem to be a bit intimidated by the dark. He's so sure- footed, and marches straight ahead. Sweet Abraham... My Sweet Abraham.

Suddenly, we're in the light again. I'm baffled.

"What was that? Lord, what *was* that?" Truthfully, I'm a bit bug-eyed now.

Jesus begins to tell me, "In all situations, you must follow My voice. Only My voice. When it looks dark, and you can't understand everything around you, keep the faith and follow My voice."

"Lord, I want to know You more and more and more. I love Your voice. Oh, how I love Your voice."

Reflection and Revelation

In the dark situations, we must hold even more tightly to our walk of faith (represented by Abraham). We can't trust any other voices but must lean heavily on the Lord. The lesson from this vision is that dark seasons may come suddenly, but we can face them with confidence by holding onto our faith, and listening to what the Lord says. We must be diligent to guard our hearts when we're walking through moments – or years – that seem dark, evil, or confusing. The enemy will try to deceive us during trouble, lead us away from our precious Lord, and divide us from trustworthy people. We must not make any drastic moves on our own during troubling days, but instead we need to lean into Jesus.

Habakkuk 2:1-3
KJV

*1 I will stand upon my watch, and set me upon the tower,
and will watch to see what he will say unto me,
and what I shall answer when I am reproved.
2 And the Lord answered me, and said,
Write the vision, and make it plain upon tables,
that he may run that readeth it.
3 For the vision is yet for an appointed time,
but at the end it shall speak,
and not lie: though it tarry, wait for it;
because it will surely come, it will not tarry.*

~ Journal Entry Day 18 ~

— Intercession Assignment —

TODAY AGAIN, I pray for my family and friends, and so many needs. Then I take time to worship the Lord, and I wait.

Jesus rides in front of me on His beautiful white horse and is clothed in Kingly attire. Oh my, how majestic and regal He is, in that golden crown and robe. Then the most astonishing thing happens: He hoists me up behind Him on His horse. Bug-eyed me!

Cities

We travel along the trail on the side of the high mountain overlooking a deep, green valley, then dismount to walk along the pathway. Up ahead, the roadside rises on one side into a steep embankment that is higher than our heads. A tree is growing on the land above us. Far below, on the other side, is a great landscape of beautiful cities. Jesus gazes at them with intense love in His eyes. We sit for a while, enjoying the view.

Decrees of the King

All at once I notice that there are scrolls lying on the ground beside Jesus; many of them. The Lord listens and hears a cry that rises from one of the cities below. In response, He reaches down to pick up a scroll. He opens it, looks out across the vast landscape toward the city and begins to make His Kingly decree over that area. Then He looks at me and indicates that I should do the same thing. So, I say what He says. I hear the words for each city, in response to the cries rising from the immense population.

"Justice" is declared over one. "Freedom" over another. "Life! Righteousness! Clear vision!" There are so many cries for help, but each one is heard and receives a decree from the Lord. I say what He says. Then Jesus prompts an image in my mind of a medieval king's herald, who stands out on the street with an elaborate scroll unrolled. Everyone knows it's the king's scroll. The herald declares what the king has said.

"Lord, this is us. You're asking us to say what You say. Help us to hear Your words and speak what You speak. May we decree and declare what You've pronounced."

The scrolls that remain on the road go into a large basket, waiting to be unrolled, read, and declared. For this time, we are finished reading and declaring. But there is much more to be done.

The Woman's Hope and Redemption

Moments pass and when I look over at Jesus, I'm surprise to notice that He's no longer wearing the Kingly robe and crown. His hair is loose, and He's wearing regular apparel. Not only that, but He's eating an apple. *What*? Eating an apple? How startling. The tree on the bank overhead has apples on it. Jesus grins broadly and hands me one. Of course, I take it, but at the same time, my mind races back to Eve in the Garden of Eden as she took the fateful apple. My Savior just looks at me and knows exactly what I'm thinking.

"I know, Lord. It might not have been a literal apple per se."

"You know it was more than the fruit." He tells me.

He has my total attention. He handed me the apple just to bring me into this conversation and now, I'm all ears.

"They'd given in to so much more, not just an appetite. Their whole estate changed. Yes, they saw their uncovered nakedness and that was so very difficult, but a great deal more occurred." Jesus looks a bit thoughtful. "They experienced something in that moment that they'd never faced: the onslaught in their minds. When they opened the door to the enemy, their minds were assaulted with all sorts of ugly and vile things. It was terrifying for them. The battle was fierce, but they were Mine and I brought them to Me. When the decree was made that the Seed of the woman would crush satan's head, Eve was given hope."

I look at Jesus and see such warmth in His eyes and in His whole appearance now. How can anyone help but love Him?

"Lord, I'm amazed by You. Simply amazed."

Reflection and Revelation

I'm reminded of the story of Sodom & Gomorrah. The cry had gone up before the Lord, a cry for help. Every city has a cry and Sodom had reached its point of no return. Jesus allowed me to see the great expanse of cities with Him, each with a heartfelt plea for His mercy. When we heard the cry, intercession began, and the Lord's declaration was made. We must hear what the Lord is saying about a place, and when we have His word on it, we must begin to decree and declare what He says. Many times, during prayer, places will come up in our spirit with a strong burden to pray specific decrees. That is the Lord's sweet urge for us to intercede and pray His word over them. When we respond, we're praying and declaring right alongside Him. Go there with Him and pray! In this vision I saw so many scrolls on the road near us. I'm certain there must be many intercessors who will take up the scrolls of His Word and help us decree what He declares.

— Intercession Assignment —

"God, give intercessors spiritual ears to hear. Lord, please help them hear You and say what You say!"

I'm so encouraged by the insight the Lord gave me today for women. In my own simple words, Eve knew she had messed up, but when the Lord revealed His promise of redemption, she realized that Womankind would be given another chance. And we know from the Word of God that the woman chosen to bear the Seed didn't fail. Mary didn't give in to anyone or anything around her. She stood on the Word she was given, that she would give birth to God's Son. Her baby was Jesus, God's Son! She held on to that Word, that truth, and never wavered. Mary stayed true and carried the Seed Eve had been told would come. What a girl, yet what a warrior Mary was. I can see the complete picture: Eve, the first woman, was deceived, but through Mary's submission to God, Womankind was used to crush that serpent's head. Talk about a blow! Hallelujah! Woman was not deceived the second time! She didn't fail. Her seed prevailed. Jesus Christ defeated the enemy through His death and resurrection. Lift up your heads, women! God is not angry with us. Oh wow. I spend a lot of time rejoicing in worship of our amazing Savior and Lord.

Psalm 104:24-25
NKJV

²⁴ O Lord, how manifold are Your works!
In wisdom You have made them all.
The earth is full of Your possessions—
²⁵ This great and wide sea,
In which are innumerable teeming things,
Living things both small and great.

~ Journal Entry Day 19 ~

—His Wonderful Creatures —

"Lord, I worship You. With anticipation and awe, I come into Your presence. How I love spending time with You."

I Have Many

Abraham has nudged right up against me. He turns his gallant head toward me, the glorious gold mane shimmering, and the impressive forelock hanging down between his eyes. He simply sparkles.

Then Jesus is here with us. Smiling. Filling my heart with such a loving expression. He strokes Abraham and then puts a blanket on him. I think to myself, 'we're going to be riding for a while'. We mount up and start the day's journey. I have the sensation that there are many things around us as we ride. We are moving above the landscape and trees begin to fade away and then we are traveling through the clouds. The heavens and beautiful creatures glide by quickly. I turn and see that the trail we've just ridden over is a gorgeous light blue. We're definitely climbing higher.

Suddenly, another horse gallops past. He's so fast! Unexpectedly, I realize he's an amazing blue in color. As soon as I manage to embrace this sight, we halt in front of a large meadow. The lush green pasture is full of horses. Horses...magnificent, muscled steeds in colors that are beyond belief. Yellows, golds, blues... startling hues. The Lord told me on one of our previous trips that He has many horses, and this is certainly proof.

Jesus grins broadly as he looks at me and says, "You love Abraham so much, and I want you to see another part of what I've prepared."

This is an amazing sight. Abraham walks in front of me, and I get the impression that he's larger than I thought.

"Jesus, Abraham looks bigger. Has he grown?"

My Savior is smiling again. As I watch, Abraham lowers his head into an open object. I realize with a start that it's a bag... the bag Jesus told me was for Abraham, the one He hung from his neck. Here it is! He's drinking from it.

"Yes, he's growing."

I gaze in wonder; it seems impossible, but the horse is even more magnificent than ever.

Jesus lingers over the gorgeous meadow full of so many splendid horses. Heaven . . .

"Lord, is this . . . heaven? It's so beautiful." I pause for a moment, then tell Him, "I have a friend who would love this." I've teasingly told her she needs a zoo for all the animals she keeps.

He smiles and nods. "Yes, you do. Bring her here." I am thinking that I can't hardly wait to tell her about this. For a moment, Jesus looks thoughtful. "People wonder if there are animals here." He pauses as He watches the striking herd for a moment. "Why wouldn't I want *all* of my lovely creations here together?"

You could've knocked me over with a feather. Oh yeah, that's me, flattened out on the floor, stunned at this realization. "Yes!" I cheer. Nodding in total agreement, I feel almost like a little kid, moving my head so emphatically that I'm in danger of falling over.

The Lord shows me a vast number of different animals; so many, so diverse and wonderfully made. A huge lion approaches:

he's almost as tall as I am! He's definitely a lion, yet so gentle and soft to the touch. Jesus strokes the massive cat's head and enormous mane. All at once, the lion roars, much to Jesus' delight. I can see He truly loves it. He even opens His mouth, roars right along with the big cat, then laughs with delight. The realization hits me again: Jesus created the sounds made by every single living thing. He taught them! He. Taught. Them. Get that!

Next, the breathtaking collection of animals unite their voices together in a glorious symphony to Jesus, their Creator. I recall the deep, loving way He'd said, 'why wouldn't I want them here?' Oh my.

"Indeed Lord. Why not?"

My mind is screaming, 'Yes, Lord! Yes, Lord!' My Savior has shown me Heaven. His Heaven. And just a small part at that. Am I even capable of saying that this is love through and through, pure love? This place, these creatures; they love. It's perfect peace. He is perfect.

"Jesus, how I love You! How great and wonderful You are!" I'm smiling so big now. "Dear Lord, I simply can't wait to tell others: animals are here!"

Reflection and Revelation

Abraham is growing! Wow. After I write down each day's experiences, I go back and read them. Each time, I gain a deeper understanding and interpretation of what I've seen. Abraham is growing. He's drinking from the bag of water which I'd understood to be the water of the Word. This means to me that my walk of faith grows when I spend time in the Word. It's food for my spirit. I think Jesus wanted to have a joyful time of allowing me to see just a tiny part of His glorious creation. The Lord's love for us is beyond our wildest imagination. He's so anxious to have us with Him. How He loves. Oh, how He loves!

2 Corinthians 10:4-5
KJV

4 For the weapons of our warfare are not carnal but mighty in God for pulling down strongholds, 5 casting down imaginations, and every high thing that exalts itself against the knowledge of God, and bringing into captivity every thought to the obedience of Christ.

~ Journal Entry Day 20 ~

—Renewing My Mind—

I HAVE FINISHED my time of worship and prayer and now...

I wait before the Lord, willing to experience whatever He wishes.

Jesus is reaching downward to lift a door open. To me, it looks like it might be flat on the floor, yet it isn't. He starts walking down what appears to be a stairway into a room, and I follow. The light for the area comes from Him.

The Old Man

There are plenty of items in the space, but what catches my attention is a frail, wrinkled, old man sitting over against one wall.

"What is this, Lord? Where are we?"

He lets me ponder on that for a moment, and I wonder about the old man. He looks as if he might be over 100 years old. Do I smile at him? Do we talk to him? What do we do?

Jesus answered, "No, we don't talk with him. He represents your old way of thinking."

Thought Patterns

"This man is symbolic of your thoughts," Jesus continues. "Remember 'the renewing of your mind'? (*Ephesians 4:22-24*) Some of your old thought patterns need to change. If they're allowed to remain, they'll grow roots and become more difficult to alter. Remember the vines?"

"Yes, Lord. I remember." My mind goes back to the time that the vines had tried to tangle themselves around my ankles and would have kept me from moving forward on my journey. Wow.

"Remove old thinking. Bring it into captivity and get rid of it." Oh, yes Lord. I must take hold of these thoughts by stopping them before they grow to bigger and bigger thoughts. I know now that some of these old thoughts are going to have to change. Jesus is telling me very simply to take control of the old thoughts that are not life-giving and remove them.

So, we're throwing the 'old man' out of here? Yep, we sure are! Out he goes! Goodbye to the old way of thinking and hello to the thinking that is rooted in God's truth.

Boxes and Crates

All around us are boxes–stacks of dusty boxes. These do not have the look of the boxes that were all packed up and marked for traveling on the road. They have the look of an old cardboard storage box, like in an attic, just gathering dust. There isn't a huge amount of them but there are several stacked up.

"Lord, what are all these crates and boxes?"

Jesus answered, "These are thoughts that you haven't unpacked yet. The enemy has slid them into your mind when you weren't aware. You haven't given them much time so far, but they're still dangerous. If you start thinking too long, lingering on them, unpacking them, then they too will grow roots and cause you much harm."

"Jesus, help me remove these thoughts. I want them out of here!"

Together, my Savior and I start cleaning up the unwanted thoughts. I see the thought of unworthiness. It's time for it to move. It is not life. So, I begin to find the scripture on how Jesus makes us worthy because of His sacrifice. He covers us with HIS worthiness. Each thought that is contrary to Jesus' character, I begin to pray and ask Jesus to wash it clean with His blood. I lean on the scripture "if *we confess our sins, He is faithful to forgive us our sins and cleanse us from all unrighteousness." (1 John 1:9 NKJV)* I clean up these boxes and clear them out. I ask Jesus to wash and cleanse every spot. I know His blood is the only thing that will wash us clean. It is the power of the blood that gives us the victory over the enemy that wars against our minds. I can take every thought to Jesus in prayer, and with the precious sacrifice that He made at the cross, I can claim the power of His blood over it.

Everything is now looking white. I'm given a cloth to wipe down every spot and declaring Jesus' blood over everything. Thank you so much Jesus, for your precious blood that washes us clean from our sin. 1 John 1:9 tells me so clearly if I just confess my sin, You are faithful. Thank you, Jesus. I'm reminded of *2 Corinthians 10:5 NKJV, "Casting down vain imaginations, and every high thing that exalts itself against the knowledge of God and bringing into captivity every thought to the obedience of Christ."* Cleansing and renewing my mind are necessary to keep me free of old habits and thoughts that don't reflect my relationship with Jesus. I must guard my mind. *Philippians 4:8 NKJV* tells me how to keep my *mind "Finally brethren, whatever things are true, whatever things are noble, whatever things are just, whatever things are pure, whatever things are lovely, whatever things are of good report, if there is any virtue and if there is anything that is praiseworthy – meditate on these things."*

After we finish clearing the boxes away, Abraham walks right up to me and (if this sounds crazy, oh well . . .) I believe he hugs me. He bends his neck and wraps his head sort of around me. I can feel that soft golden mane on my skin.

"Thank You, precious Jesus. You know I needed that."

Reflection and Revelation

Later in the afternoon I drove to pick up my grandchildren from school. While waiting in line in my car, I turned on the radio for a few minutes. Immediately, I heard the program host introducing a woman author, Jennie Allen. Her book is entitled, "Get Out of Your Head: Stopping the Spiral of Toxic Thoughts."[9] I was floored as these two people discussed the dangerous thought patterns in our minds.

I'm absolutely in awe of our God. Talk about a confirmation! I'm ordering her book. Wow. We need our Lord to help us guard our minds. The enemy (satan) will come with a fleeting thought, suspicion, lie or twisted truth, and if we dwell on those, we'll begin to believe them, and they'll cause us trouble. We must learn to recognize his sneaky ways, and not give in to that ole cunning voice trying to turn our head and then our heart in a direction that's not the way of the Lord. Think about times when thoughts of discontentment, distrust, arguing, or hatred enter your mind. The old way of thinking, represented by that old man, must be cleaned out, and a 'new man', with Christ-like thoughts and new ways needs to emerge.

We are told in *2 Corinthians 5:17 "Therefore if any man be in Christ, he is a <u>new creature</u>: <u>old</u> things are passed away; behold, all things are become new."* This is a beautiful picture of our new birth in Christ Jesus! We are a brand-new person! *A new man!* Now with our NEW man, OLD ways, OLD things are behind us and a brand-new way of life is before us. Hallelujah! Thank you for the NEW!

Jeremiah 29:11
NIV

*11 For I know the plans I have for you," declares the L*ord*,
"plans to prosper you and not to harm you,
plans to give you hope and a future.*

~ Journal Entry Day 21 ~

—Intercession Calling—

I'M MORE AND more drawn to my precious time with Jesus; His presence is irresistible. Yes, my time is valuable, but sharing the first moments of my day with Him is worth it to me. This morning I wait before Him with great anticipation.

The Urgency of Intercession

Abraham approaches, clearly larger than ever. What looks like a large white blanket is rolled up on his back. The stallion is full frontal and galloping hard toward me.

"He loves this! Go Abraham!" I hear Jesus urging him onward.

As Jesus charges near on his fabulous steed, He reaches out and grabs my hand to swing me up on Abraham's back. We race forward, flying at top speed. I notice there's a drape of very familiar material laid out, just behind the head of His horse. It's our American flag.

We ride up and up through the sky into the heavens and Jesus unfurls the flag. I watch as the striking emblem of our country gracefully unrolls and ripples in the Wind. There it is, suspended in the heavens.

"I declare a thing to be," the Lord proclaims, "and it will be. America *shall not* fall."

Our banner of freedom is stretched out in the cosmos, a waving symbol of this decree.

Sharing Our Prayer Shawl with Jesus

Next, we're sitting right on top of a huge mountain peak that overlooks a massive landscape. It seems as if we can see the entire world just from this spot. Even huge mountains seem to appear small from this high peak. Abraham comes near, and I notice that the rolled white blanket that was on his back is now stretched out over us. It reminds me of a Jewish prayer shawl, and it covers both me and Jesus. Prayer shawls are so precious. I know that it is the Jewish men that cover themselves with the shawl in a time of prayer and meditation. The beautiful bands of color symbolize nobility – children of the Greatest King. Even the tassels were a sign of obedience to God and His laws. But today, we see them in so many of our own Christian churches. They have taken on a meaning to us that means– by covering ourselves we are closing ourselves off from everything else and focusing entirely on Him. Like, wrapping ourselves up in His presence. Now, here my precious Lord has extended it over me. The time I spend with Him in prayer is very special. It's a marvelous privilege for me to declare what He says, especially when I know He's right here beside me. What a tremendous thought: the Lord of the universe sits beside me when I pray.

Future

A very unique horse approaches: I've never seen anything like it. He's completely covered with transparent gold mirrors of multiple shapes and sizes, a life-size multi-faceted golden gemstone. It is incredibly beautiful and unique.

"What is this, Lord?"

"This is Future. He doesn't go in the meadow with the other horses. I Am the only one Who rides him. Actually, I hold him together. See the gold? That's Me. I hold the Future." Jesus answers.

I think to myself that the beautiful shining gold must be His glory; it's as bright as the morning sun.

Jesus proceeds, "You wonder why so many people see so many different things for the Future. It's because each individual sees a different facet of Future's appearance."

He waits and lets me look and absorb this.

"Are you afraid of Future?" Jesus is looking at the horse.

"No, I'm not," I reply with confidence. "How could I fear something so incredibly beautiful when I'm here with You, Jesus, in perfect peace?"

"Never be afraid of the Future; I'm there."

Reflection and Revelation

Our sweet homeland is struggling. Followers of Jesus are being drawn into a time of interceding for America. We can trust that He will prompt us when to pray, and how. In this vision, Abraham was running swiftly and that indicates to me that the hour is late, and intercession is urgently needed.

The golden horse Future totally amazed me. Only Jesus holds our future. What peace that brings! We should never fear if Jesus is already ahead of us, there in our future. In this earthly life, there are so many difficult moments, and sometimes darkness seems to be all around. But in my time of prayer, Jesus allowed me to see that no matter what challenges we face, He is right beside us and always will be. Our sweet Savior holds the Future. Why should we worry when He is there?

Revelation 22:16 NKJV "I am the Alpha and the Omega, the Beginning and the End, the First and the Last."

Amen Lord! Amen!

Psalm 122:6
KJV

Pray for the peace of Jerusalem:
they shall prosper that love thee.

~ Journal Entry Day 22 ~

—Intercession Assignment—

Lord, I run to You and Your presence. I wait before you.

Jerusalem

I see Jesus' face and there are tears flowing like a waterfall from His eyes. He reaches out to take my hand and leads me toward a globe, our Earth. We hover together over Jerusalem, over Israel.

"Lord, my heart is Your heart. I weep with You."

He's bent over this precious place, and I begin to cry out for Jerusalem and her peace. I pray for protection from the enemy that is trying to destroy her.

"I Am her 'dome' of protection."

"They depend on that dome, but Jesus *You* are their true covering.' The Iron Dome is part of Israel's defense system that is used to intercept incoming short-range rockets. I hear it in the news often, but I see Jesus as He is the true one hovering over Israel as her true protector. Yes, He is their true dome of protection.

Crying with my Savior, I pray with urgency for there to be peace in Jerusalem, for their eyes to see Jesus as their Messiah. In agreement with the promises in God's Word, I declare peace and fervently intercede for them.

Then I hear Him say, "I must be their Savior before I can be their King."

I pray even more for the salvation of the people of Israel. Watching from Heaven with Jesus, I can see they weep at the Wailing Wall, poking paper with their written prayers into its cracks and crevices. I ask God to open their eyes, so they can see Jesus as their Savior and King, and know He is there with them.

The Sword of Peace

A long, bright, sharp sword appears. There's something odd about it; does it really have flowers on the handle? I'm a bit puzzled about that but reach out and take hold of it anyway. Abraham gallops toward me and he is absolutely massive; his muscles are bulging! Suddenly I'm riding him with my sword in hand, charging forward. I see now that Abraham is wearing armor. We're in warfare, evidently.

"Lord, I follow Your command. I declare the Word You have spoken over the people of Israel. They will inherit every promise made to them. I'm praying that they will all receive You as their Savior and Lord. Salvation for Israel!" I shout. "Salvation! And I declare Your Kingdom will come. I hold firmly to this promise and declare it with You, Lord."

Of course, my curious mind is always working to grasp the meaning of my experiences, so when we stop, I ask Jesus about something I still don't understand.

"Help me figure out the sword, Lord. It has flowers on the handle, which doesn't seem to fit. I mean, here's Abraham looking all massive with muscles bulging, charging forward wearing battle armor. And I'm riding him, holding a big, sharp sword, but it has a handle of flowers."

My mind is reeling. Immediately, Jesus shows me flowers falling over the map of Jerusalem.

"It's the sword of peace."

I'm wielding the sword of peace. I cry out again for the peace of Jerusalem. Pray with me that Jesus' declaration will come true soon.

Reflection and Revelation

The declaration over Jerusalem is evidently one that we must "suit up" for, a decree from the heart of a warrior. The ancient covenant with God has been on a battlefield throughout the ages. But in the spirit, we can proclaim what Jesus' heart is. Pray for Jerusalem, for peace there. How could a sword be linked with peace? When I see the sword that has a handle overlaid with flowers, I must conclude that the flowers falling from this sword were the prayers that we pray for her peace.

When I intercede for that city, I pray for safety and protection from war and enemies that want to destroy her. But I'm seeing something deeper here: Jesus is their only true peace. I pray for their eyes to see Him, their true Peace, The Prince of Peace.

1 Peter 4:7
KJV

But the end of all things is at hand:
be ye therefore sober, and WATCH unto prayer.

Colossians 4: 2
KJV

Continue in prayer and watch in the same with thanksgiving.

~ Journal Entry Day 23 ~

—The Watchtower – Insights for Watchmen—

I COME TO my prayer time not knowing if there's anything You'll show me. In total surrender, I come before You, submitting to whatever You wish to show or not show me. How I love Your presence! You're so good, and I worship You, delighted to spend this time waiting for You.

The Watchmen Assignment

Jesus rides toward me astride his brilliant white horse. When they come to a stop, He dismounts and retrieves an object from His saddle bag. The more He unfolds it, the bigger it gets. The tremendous item cascades down a mountainside and across a tree-scattered landscape toward a tower in the distance. I gaze across the land and realize the construction is a bridge. Together, we cross it, heading in the direction of the tower. As we travel, the Lord talks about the Watch Tower. I remember studying the function of watch towers and the watchmen stationed in them. When we arrive and climb to the top of the lookout, I notice there's a mist obscuring our view of the panorama below.
"What is this, Lord?"

Levels of the Watchtower

Jesus guides me down a stairway inside the tower to another level. As we look out the window there, I can clearly see everything below the cloud, as well as what's causing it. Two atmospheres are interacting: holy above and evil below. The misty fog exists because of the deployment of evil forces sent to cause trouble. I know I can call on Jesus to send angel armies to help us.

All the activity can't be seen from just one level. The watchtower has an upper floor that enables me to see from above the cloud, and a lower floor that allows me to see the activity beneath it. What a glorious blessing!

Reflection and Revelation

The watchmen on the wall are intercessors, people who are called to watch and pray. These spiritual warriors often experience a two-sided word from the Lord. God allows them to be aware of the works of the enemy from different levels and assigns them to pray according to what they've seen and heard from Him. This is a powerful illustration. Precision prayer, focused directly on the need, is necessary. As I meditate on this, I realize that not only will the watchmen see the evil forces attack, but they'll also be able to see the glory of God at work. Watchmen receive alerts about the need for prayer, but they also see the glory of God as it settles over the site of that warfare. We must stay alert and 'watch and pray' as Jesus commanded.[10] The Lord will guide us when we are interceding as watchmen on the tower, showing us the necessity for prayer and the cause of that need.

Matthew 9:37
KJV

*37 Then saith He unto His disciples,
the harvest truly is plenteous, but the laborers are few;
38 Pray ye therefore the Lord of the harvest,
that He will send forth laborers into His harvest.*

~ Journal Entry Day ~ 24

—Assignment for the Harvest—

AFTER A TIME of prayer, I wait, and a vision begins to open before me.

I see Jesus, His brilliant white horse, and Abraham. My beautiful Savior reaches out to me, smiling and without condemnation. He has missed our times together. Oh my, I have too! So much has been happening: sicknesses, deaths, work. So many life situations have kept me on the run, and I've missed a few days of truly coming into His presence. I've prayed, of course, but I'm referring to my secret place time alone with Him. Bringing my attention to my phone, He gently reminds me that His voice is what I need.

"Oh, Jesus, You are all I need. Forgive me, please."

There stands sweet Abraham. I reach out to touch the softness of his gold mane and take just a brief moment to hug him.

The Fields

Then I turn to look around. We're standing in a large field. There are no mountains, just flat land and a few trees in the distance. We're in the middle of acres of beautiful golden wheat. I look at Jesus and think, 'What?'

"The Harvest, Kathy. Look, the Harvest is ready." He sweeps His arm broadly over the vast expanse. I look again and see what seem to be miles and miles of this gorgeous gold grain stretched out before me, glistening in the sunlight. The Wind sweeps over the crop in gentle waves, and I can smell the grain.

The Harvesters

Then I see a huge harvester, or combine tractor, and hear the roar of its mighty engine as it gathers in giant amounts of wheat. This massive machine cuts probably 20 to 30, maybe even 40 rows of wheat in one swipe. I'm aware there's more than one of them.

Jesus tells me, "These are the harvesters I've prepared to gather the ripened crop. I've developed and equipped them to bring in thousands, even millions, at a time. They're mine." Yes Lord, these huge harvesters are Yours and they are gathering in Your harvest. I watch the breathtaking feat.

"But look again." He spoke.

The Ones That Remained

I can see that the immense tractor didn't gather every single stalk of the grain. Scattered throughout the field and along the edges are smaller amounts of grain that have been left behind.

The Ruths

"Remember Ruth," He says, "and the gleaners who gathered by hand what the harvesters missed."[11]

"Yes Lord, I do remember." I have the deep feeling that I'm seeing a harvest of the souls of men.

"The whole world is being prepared. Get ready to gather in the harvest of people. Don't get weary in the place where you are. Gather the few; I want them all. It's the desire of My heart, the Father's heart, and the heart of the Holy Spirit, for every single human being to be saved and gathered into relationship with Us.

Many of My followers are fervently working to gather them. We see every single stalk."

Reflection and Revelation

Many people avoid large crowds and won't attend a 'big tractor event' with thousands and millions of others. Perhaps they're shy or anxious, yet they need to be reached. Jesus showed me that He has prepared the Ruths, the gleaners, to gather each person gracefully and carefully.

The precious Holy Spirit is moving over the world to save those who are lost, just like the Wind I saw sweeping over the field of grain. He's been moving the Harvest into readiness. And now He quickens the hearts of the large ministries (tractors) to reach many, and of the smaller ministries (gleaners) to gather those which the large ones will never reach. They are equally important and equally called by the Lord of the Harvest. Every single person is sought by our heavenly Father. His heart is ever reaching to gather them to Himself.

"Lord, in whatever place You have me, help me to reach the lost. Help me to encourage others to reach out and bring in this harvest."

As the harvest vision fades, another begins.

The Dividing

Jesus is riding His horse swiftly at the front of a lightning bolt that is shooting across the sky. Abraham gallops up behind Jesus, beaming with a bright light. His mane is almost glowing it's so bright.

"Quickly, get on!" Jesus' voice is urgent.

I mount my horse and discover we're riding on this flash of lightning! The Lord is out front, and the lightning bolt follows

Him. I don't know how, but I follow. Then the knowledge hits me: Father God has sent His Word and we're riding on it. Then Jesus stops his horse and tells me to watch. We're suspended in space on the lightning bolt. It changes direction and strikes downward, hitting the earth below us. Is it going to hit a city? Jesus tells me to keep watching. The shaft hits the ground and from that spot an earthquake divides the land we can see below.

"Kathy, do you see? It divides. See the earth has shifted into two sides."

"Yes, Lord," I murmur. "I see."

Reflection and Revelation

My heart was stirred as I watched the bolt of lightning hit the earth. I pondered it for some time. Is there a time when Earth will experience an earthquake that devastating? The Bible book of Revelation speaks of earthquakes that are coming. It makes me wonder if I'm seeing that which is to come.

The Word is quick and powerful, and sharper than any two-edged sword. (Hebrews 4:12) When His Word goes out, people have the choice to receive it or refuse it. It's that simple. There's not an in between answer. It divides the truth from the lie, belief from unbelief. It's sharp enough to split bone from marrow and separate people who have accepted the Lord from those who haVen't. Be aware that the Word doesn't always unite. Sometimes It divides.

This reminds me of *Joshua 24:15 NKJV* *"Choose you this day whom ye will serve; whether the gods which your fathers served that were on the other side of the flood, or the gods of the Amorites, in whose land ye dwell: but as for me and my house, we will serve the Lord."*

Choose Life. Choose Jesus. Choose to serve our precious Savior.

Kingdom Placement, Kingdom Equipping & Kingdom Protocol

Ephesians 4:16
NKJV

*16 From whom the whole body joined and knit together
by what which every joint supplies,
according to the effectual working by which
every part does its share,
causes growth of the body unto the edifying of itself in love.*

~ Journal Entry Day 25 ~

—Kingdom Placement and Equipping—

I'VE SPENT MY time in prayer and worship, and as I wait a vision begins . . .

Kingdom Placement

Jesus is on His horse, pulling something behind Him. It's not exactly a wagon, but something with wheels; maybe a cart. I follow on Abraham, stroking his head.

Jesus looks back and smiles, "You love Abraham, don't you?"

"I love *You*, Lord. Every moment with You and everything You give is precious to me, and Abraham is one of Your gifts. Yes, Lord, I do love him."

We travel along a mountainside overlooking a town. Jesus dismounts and turns to the cart, which has a large bag on it. As He opens the bag, I can see several objects inside it. There are intricately detailed blueprints laid out on unique paper which He unfolds. It's the plan for the city. Jesus pulls another object from the bag. As I study the round, clear glass, framed with gold filigree, I realize it's a magnifying glass. I know that it will magnify and illuminate smaller things when light shines through it. Next Jesus pulls a watch tower from the bag, and meticulously places it in the town below, along with all the other items. There is a well, or fountain of water at the end of one of the streets. As I continue to watch, He places lamp posts along the lanes to light the way to the well. Each piece is carefully and strategically placed in the city. Just watching Him, I know it is a well-designed layout.

"What is this?" I ask. "What am I seeing?"

Then the scripture comes to mind. Of course! This is a picture of the teachings from the book of Ephesians about the way the Body of Christ has been fashioned. Every person is placed in the Body by Him, specially designed to work cooperatively together, each person doing their part. Jesus is placing each item in the town of my vision, representing the way He places each individual in the Church to accomplish a specific purpose. The scripture fills me with a new desire to do my part in fulfilling God's plan. The people of this heavenly town depend on the watch tower to warn them of impending danger or even of coming blessings. They can rely on the lamp posts for guiding light and the well for life-giving water. Even the magnifying glass is necessary for highlighting the smaller details that need attention. The Light shines through it to reveal what needs to be seen. Wow.

The Lord then allows me to see just a small glimpse of something much more personal. Just for a moment, I see my dad. He's young and not wearing glasses; I don't know if I'd ever seen him without them. Dad is smiling so big. He's getting ready to BBQ for us! *What?* Can we do that in heaven? Only Jesus knows how special this is to me. Dad loved having all the family at his house and enjoyed getting out the grill. It was a big family event for us, and we loved it. What a wonderful surprise. The things that bring us joy are waiting for us. What a sweet moment, to get to see just a tiny part of the happiness in store. He loves us so much. God loves us so very much.

—Kingdom Placement and Equipping—

Let Me Linger Longer

"I've learned so much just seeing this town. My spirit is so full, and I just don't want to leave You. Lord, I long to be here with You, to stay awhile."

Jesus is seated, and I'm sitting beside Him, at His feet where I can lean on Him. He puts His hand on the back of my head. My heart is so full, just to be right here next to my Savior. His presence is life. The Lord points into the distance, and then I can see afar off.

"What I'm preparing . . ." he says.

I can hear the sound of people. They're getting everything ready for our arrival. It sounds like the arrangements for a big party. The Father is preparing a celebration!

Reflection and Revelation

This vision gave me an even greater determination to fill my place in the Church, the Body God has designed, and stay faithful. Each piece in the town was so important, just as each person is needed in the Church. If we are each a part, and He is strategically placing us exactly where we're needed, what happens if we move too quickly, too slowly, or out of our place?

What is my place in the Kingdom? I follow Him and whatever assignment He has for me; that's how I serve His purpose and plan. Do we even realize that our life and contributions have purpose in the Kingdom of God? Do we comprehend that our destiny is a strategic placement by the King? I pray that God will help us to fill our unique spot and motivate us to be faithful in our Kingdom assignment. Your spot in the Kingdom may be teaching or preaching, but there are a great many other ways to make the Church complete. Every single piece is necessary. I remember when Jesus said, "*. . . when the Son of Man comes* *will He really find faith on the earth?"*[12] Could that possibly be "faithfulness"? It's a thought worth our time to ponder.

"Lord, help me to recognize where I belong and stay put in the spot where You've placed me. Help me be committed to my calling. I pray now for faithfulness among Your Body of people. Holy Spirit, help us to serve You with dedication."

1 Corinthians 2:9-10
NKJV

*9 But as it is written, Eye has not seen, nor ear heard,
nor have entered into the heart of man,
the things which God has prepared for those who love him.
10 But God has revealed them to us through His Spirit:
For the Spirit searches all things, yes, the deep things of God.*

~ Journal Entry Day 26 ~

—Kingdom Equipping—

"TODAY I WAIT before You. I need Your presence, and just want to spend time right here with You."

Jesus and I are sitting in front of a campfire. I can lean on Him, perfectly content to be right here, soaking in His wonderful presence. The fire warms me to my innermost being, like healing love flowing through. Oh, I know that sweet Holy Spirit fire.

The Library of Books and Resources

After a long while, Jesus says He wants to show me His library.

"Library? Did You say, 'library'?" Amazed, I'm working to absorb that thought. He has a library...

In the next moment, He's leading me through an enormous gallery. It is exquisite, exceedingly high and full of light. The atmosphere is so bright, I wonder if it even has a roof. There are big chairs, tables and of course, books; so many books! Rows and rows of bookshelves are filled with incredible volumes. It's almost beyond my ability to grasp what I'm seeing.

"The publications here contain only the truth. Every book inspired by the Father, Son, and Holy Spirit is kept in this holy place. Books penned by authors throughout all the ages are here, and truth is what is coming forth from them. If the writers on Earth missed it a little, here in heaven, the truth is revealed and recorded as it was intended."

Awestruck, I learn that I can meet the authors and listen to them talk about their books and their experiences. This is so incredible! I'm allowed to speak with authors from any era of the Earth. Unbelievably, there's the opportunity to open the books and see them the way the authors saw them in their imagination. It's difficult to explain the way I can experience what caused the books to be written as though I was there in the life of the author when they were writing.

I ask Jesus about the Bible and the authors who heard the voice of the Lord and were inspired to write what He said. I can actually see that happening! The Bible is held in a very special place, but I'm able to look at it. The prophets are here and talk to me about their writings. They answer questions I have about how they felt as they tried to pen the awesomeness of God's very Word.

There's even a kids' section. That's almost more than I can absorb. Children are here reading… and astoundingly, the books are talking back to them! They can interact with the books like living creatures. It's as if the stories pop up in live action when they're being read. Their little hands lovingly stroke the pages. What a wonderfully exciting place for these children.

Art and Music

The Lord takes me further into this massive structure of buildings to see artists and their works. I'm simply blown away. The artists are still painting and creating, taught by the Holy Spirit. Whatever is in their heart to make, He empowers them. What a magnificent, massive gallery.

There are no words big enough to describe the music. Every sound, every instrument is overwhelmingly beautiful. The musicians are completely absorbed in worship, an indescribable honoring of the Lord. I can actually see the sound; it looks like a

Wind, Holy Spirit Wind, and it swirls around the musicians, taking them up as they play in the Spirit. People are dancing and rejoicing in this incredibly amazing symphony of sounds.

Jesus is having a huge time with this. Father God and the Holy Spirit are totally enjoying watching and interacting with everyone. It's one big joyful expression of Him. Every piece of art, every single note in the songs is all about Him and His love. It brings healing and warmth and love to my very soul. The expressions of worship are glorious, and He is splendid, basking in this adoration. I'm so overcome. How can we not want to spend our eternity here with Him? He's so incredibly amazing. Love is everywhere here. There's not one single spot that lacks love and peace. Such marvelous peace. What astounding love. Oh my! I never want to be without my sweet Jesus, my Savior. He is my everything.

Reflection and Revelation

I wanted to share this journal entry because it revealed to me that our God has so much more prepared for us than we can even begin to think. It's endless! There's no possibility of being bored in heaven; none. This makes me want to go there more than anything. Nothing is worth losing our beautiful relationship with Jesus. Words can't do it justice, but maybe you can see just a small part, as I have, and your love for Him will grow.

Romans 12:6-8
KJV

6 Having then gifts differing according to the grace that is given to us, whether prophecy, let us prophesy according to the proportion of faith;

7 Or ministry, let us waiteth on our ministering: or he that teacheth, on teaching;

8 Or he that exhorteth, on exhortation: he that giveth, let him do it with simplicity; he that ruleth, with diligence; he that sheweth mercy, with cheerfulness.

1 Corinthians 12:4-11
KJV

4 Now there are diversities of gifts, but the same Spirit.

5 And there are differences of administrations, but the same Lord.

6 And there are diversities of operations, but it is the same God which worketh all in all.

7 But the manifestation of the Spirit is given to every man to profit withal.

8 For to one is given by the Spirit the word of wisdom; to another the word of knowledge by the same Spirit;

9 To another faith by the same Spirit; to another the gifts of healing by the same Spirit;

10 To another the working of miracles; to another prophesy; to another discerning of spirits; to another divers kinds of tongues; to another the interpretation of tongues:

11 But all these worketh that one and the selfsame Spirit, dividing to every man severally as he will.

~ Journal Entry Day 27 ~

— Equipping: Giftings —

MY TIME OF worship and prayer leads into the time of waiting before Him.

Jesus is looking out an earthly-style window with glass panes. "Come look with Me." He speaks.

I try to look out through the window.

"Lord, I can't see anything."

He looks at me and reaches over to hold my head. He put a hand on each side of my face and He moves my head again to look through the window with His help.

"I've anointed your eyes. You *can* see. Look."

Once again, I peer through the glass, but turn toward Him for a moment to see where He's gazing. It's so hard to turn away from His beautiful face and look back out the window. I struggle to tear my gaze away from Him, but then do as He has bidden.

The Shoreline

Our surroundings become clearer, and I notice that the window is set in the thick wall of a huge stone building situated by the sea. It feels like I imagine a castle would; tall and fortified. From our vantage point, I can see the beach and the hear the water as it rolls to the shore in gentle waves. The Lord points, and I'm able to pick out a large ship far off in the distance. Somehow, I know the vessel is searching for a place to anchor near land. I'm also aware that some of the inlets along this coastline are dangerously full of coral reefs and sharp rocks that could damage the bottom of the ship. It's drawing nearer, and from our high perspective, I anxiously search the blue green water closest to our building. What a relief to see only the soft seaweed gently flowing back and forth with the waves.

The Net

Oh! I grin broadly with excitement; the ship can land here safely. As it draws near, the crew lowers huge nets. Jesus and I walk down to the beach to see in greater detail. I wonder at the use of nets so close to land. They're stretched out like a plank would've been, which causes me to question the procedure. Large crates are then hoisted over the side of the ship; they glide gracefully down the nets without difficulty.

"Lord, why are they using these immense nets instead of a gangplank?"

"These are the same nets they use for fishing." He answered.

Still uncertain, I'm left to contemplate and a bit later I converse with Jesus a little more deeply.

Reflection and Revelation

I learn from further probing that the ship unloading crates represents the Holy Spirit searching for a place to bestow His gifts. The ability to receive what He offers comes through the same faith we activate in order to receive Jesus. We come by faith because Holy Spirit draws us, attracting us to Christ. He 'catches' us in the net of His love and we receive Him by faith. I'm so very grateful!

Our sweet Holy Spirit watches us to see where our shoreline of readiness can receive more from Him. Our giftings come from Him. (See Romans 12 and 1 Corinthians 12).

— Equipping: Giftings —

We can't receive His gifts if our hearts are hard and crusty like coral. We must guard our actions, so we aren't sharp, but tender and merciful.

"Lord, help us not to get crusty and set in our ways, or to live in any fashion that would make it difficult to receive the gifts from Your hand. Help our hearts to stay humble and tender before You."

John 6:50-51
NKJV

⁵⁰ This is the bread which comes down from heaven, that one may eat of it and not die.
⁵¹ I am the living bread which came down from heaven: if anyone eats of this bread, he will live forever: and the bread that I shall give is My flesh, which I shall give for the life of the world.

~ Journal Entry Day 28 ~

— Feeding the Multitudes —

"Jesus, I love You so much, and deeply desire this time with You. Everything about You is precious to me." Waiting for time with Him is such a privilege and honor. "Lord," I whisper. "What's in Your heart today? I'm open to anything You desire."

My Lord and I are walking by the sea. I feel sand under my bare feet and look to see that He is barefoot too. Wow, I think, "Jesus' feet in the sand…"

Immediately He responds, "Yes, I love to feel the sand too."

It's still so amazing to me that He knows my thoughts and then just answers me. The realization isn't new, but this experience with Him being visibly beside me is incredible.

"Lord, I love what You've created. Even the seashells are amazingly beautiful, each one unique. I've collected them on earth for years. What a wonderful Designer You are!"

We're just walking along, enjoying the sand, sunshine, water, and playful breezes, but my mind is at work.

"Jesus, I know You fed fish to the multitude, and I've wondered what it must've been like to eat fish from Your hand." I'm smiling blissfully just thinking about it.

He nods and grins, "It was a good day."

We wander toward a nearby hillside beside the sea, and Jesus talks to me about that day of the thousands.[13]

I'm almost gushing out the words, "Oh Lord! I *love* this part of scripture! I've always enjoyed picturing You and your disciples with all those people."

"You think Peter was the boisterous one? Well, he surely was joyful that day, but *John* was the one bouncing around." He laughs and continues. "He was having such a great time."

I can see my Savior is enjoying the memory. Wow. Then He murmurs rather wistfully, "It was a good day... even for Judas." He pauses for a moment. "He was amazed." We're both absorbed in this thought for a moment. Judas.

The Deeper Word

Then He starts again. "Oh, I know My brothers loved every minute of serving the people. The crowd really enjoyed the fish and even came back for more the next day. But when they discovered there was no more to eat, they all walked away. I even asked My own disciples if they were going to leave Me too. Oh, but I knew they wouldn't follow Me for long just for the fish; they needed the deeper Me. They needed the eternal."

The Lord gazes out over the surrounding scenery. "It's like this: do you remember when your Dad told you 'if one person can get them with a hot dog someone else will come along and win them with a hamburger'?"

Oh wow! I giggle. Yes! I haven't thought of that in a long time. I remember Dad saying that very thing many times while he was preaching. Dad was talking about people being lured away from church with the promise of entertainment and hotdogs. My Dad didn't mince words.

Jesus chuckled, "I loved that! He was such a fireball! I gave him the thought, and he just put it out there." He grins broadly and turns to me. "Do you understand? If the people only wanted the fish, they would've totally missed Me. A few went home and thought it through, then came back to Me. But so many didn't. They couldn't handle the deeper Me. When I said, 'Eat of My flesh and drink of My blood,' their brains couldn't receive the symbolism. But I knew they had to follow Me to the place of sacrifice and receive it by faith to be free."

Now it's my turn to absorb the deeper picture. All the people in that massive crowd consumed the physical part, the fish, which filled their appetites for the moment. But most totally missed the beautiful Savior, the living Sacrifice, and the eternal life that was to come through Him. They received the miracle of the moment yet walked away from the reward of the eternal.

Fishing For a Recipe

"This is so marvelous, Lord. How I love you! Our talks, and our time together are my favorite things."

Then He smiles so big; I mean he turns and flashes such a humungous grin that it startles me.

"You wanna know what I put on the fish, don't you?" He's grinning so broadly! That grin is my undoing every single time. I'm a wreck. It blows me away, and I find myself smiling from ear to ear. No longer able to hold it in, we both burst out laughing. Oh my.

"Yes, Lord. Yes, I want to know!"

"Lemon. Mint. Parsley."

What? Did Jesus really just list off a recipe for fish?

"No garlic this time."

He *knows* I was thinking there would've been garlic. He just knows it! Then He lets me taste it. I don't know how. I can't explain it, but He does. Then He smiles so beautifully. Every time He does, it's like water to a thirsty soul. That loving expression is so good for my heart and soul.

"Lord, I just want to stay right here with You. I so love being in Your presence. Your presence, Your smile, Your voice, Your overwhelming love bring a peace to me that I've never experienced with anyone else. I never want to be without Your presence. Never."

We walk back down to the sea again, where there's a wonderful fire. For a while we sit in silence, simply gazing out across the sea. All at once, I realize that I recognize this fire; it's the healing fire of the Holy Spirit, warming me through and through. I could thank my Savior a million times for all He is and has done, and it will never be enough. I look out across the sea; the sun is shining so beautifully on the water.

"I put the sun and the moon in the sky just for you, for mankind to know times and seasons. They are a gift that continues, on and on. My lights are a constant abiding timepiece from Me."

I contemplate the sun and moon, the timepieces of the Lord. We look out across the sea and then stand and walk out into the crystal water. It's so clear at first, then shimmers like a mirror, which becomes molten silver flowing.

"Lord, how I love you!"

Reflection and Revelation

He so joyfully brings me to scripture and teaches me more and more. Oh, how marvelous to me is this time with Him. To know my Lord even more deeply is my desire. I pray that He will keep me from being like the crowd was the day He multiplied the loaves and fish, experiencing only the miracle of the moment. Truly God performs miracles, but may we never have our miracle moment only to walk away unchanged in our heart by the eternal.

The gentle reminder of His timepieces, the sun, the moon, and the heavens are there letting us know of the changing of the seasons, the movement of days and years. But oh my, they are so much more to those of us who are watching. The seasons change prophetically and occasionally, we see it in the skies. We stand and watch, waiting to see what He will say to us.

John 4:14
NKJV

¹⁴ But whoever drinks of the water that I shall give him will never thirst; but the water that I shall give him will be in him a fountain of water springing up into everlasting life.

~ Journal Entry Day 29 ~

— Go to the Thirsty —

I'VE HAD MY time of praying and interceding before the Lord. I worship and then . . . I wait.

Jesus is extending His hands toward me. Of course, I'll follow. It never occurs to me to say no to His invitations! He has a bucket in one hand; actually, He has two, because He keeps one and hands another to me. We're walking toward a well, so I immediately focus on learning what this means. We fill our buckets with water from the well. It is so easy. The well is so full the only thing we must do is simply offer our buckets and with just a simple dip, the buckets are brimming with clear cool water. Somehow, I realize this water is His presence, His everlasting well of Water spoken of in the book of *John chapter 4:10*. *"Jesus answered and said to her, 'If you knew the gift of God and who it is who says to you, 'Give Me a drink,' you would have asked Him, and He would have given you living water." KJV*

Looking nearby, I notice there are people seated on the ground, and they appear to be very parched and dry. They're obviously weak and listless, with dry, cracked lips. Even their hands and feet look depleted and dusty. My heart goes out to them. Immediately I turn to them and carefully pour Water from my bucket into each person's mouth. I want to pour it all over their face and hands, to bring relief to their poor, dried-up bodies, and souls. I think of their precious feet.

"Lord, I don't want to waste the Water; is it proper to put it on their feet? Is it ok?"

Jesus assures me there is plenty, and continually refills the bucket for me. As I quench their thirst and pour the precious liquid on their feet, I can see the sparkle begin to come back into their eyes. All these folks were so very thirsty, and they're savoring every drop.

"Lord, what does this mean? Jesus, I know You are the Fountain of life. You're this water. I'm like the bucket, filled with You so I can take You to the whole community. Jesus, I want to help, but how do I get it to them all?"

My mind is reeling, thinking of every human being on Earth, so deeply in need of Jesus. Getting the Living Water to them in the usual way is a great challenge; so many are turned off by church and church people.

Then Jesus tells me, "Go to the thirsty and the dry. Don't continue to try to fill the ones who are full and not even thirsty."

'Oh, my goodness,' I think. 'Simply go to those who are eager and craving the Water. If people are turning away from it, they're not truly thirsty.'

"I'm seeking after You, Lord to help me find those who are thirsty and parched. I want to pour this Water of life on their feet and show them how to drink from this well of You. I want to see the life come into their eyes. Your life, Lord. Please help me to recognize the truly thirsty."

Reflection and Revelation

Thoughts of all the thirsty people stay with me. I can still envision the dry, parched lips and the dehydrated hands and feet of the crowd around the well. Do we even realize that we can carry the refreshing Water to those who are longing to know the Lord? Do we know that through the power of Jesus in us, we can refresh another believer's journey by cooling his feet with refreshing of the Water of the Spirit? I pray that the Lord will keep our hearts full of His love so we can pour out to the thirsty and dry. Let's be ready at any moment to be that encouraging force. Fill up to overflowing and be ready to pour.

Ephesians 2:4-10
KJV

*[4]But God, who is rich in mercy,
for His great love wherewith He loved us,
[5]Even when we were dead in sins,
hath quickened us together with Christ,
(by grace ye are saved)
[6]And hath raised us up together,
and made us to sit together in heavenly places in Christ Jesus:
[7]That in the ages to come He might show the exceeding riches
of His grace in His kindness toward us through Christ Jesus:*

~ Journal Entry Day 30 ~

—God's Amazing Love—

EVERY TIME IN His presence is intentional. I take the time to come and pray, to worship and read His word. Then I wait. I simply wait.

As I wait in the presence of the Lord, I see Abraham wearing an elaborate headdress. Fringes of it spill over his forehead, cover the sides of his face and cascade down his neck. I'm not sure what to call this incredibly beautiful covering. It's burnished gold, embellished with shimmering gemstones: emeralds, sapphires, rubies, and diamonds. The entire adornment is so colorful, glistening and sparkling from every angle. Wow: I wonder if Abraham is heading to a big event, like the other time I saw jewels in his mane and tail. I'm riding the massive stallion now, and my attire matches his glittering appearance. The elegant robe of spun gold is embedded with the same twinkling gems, as are the glinting knee-high boots. I'm speechless with amazement, and don't know quite how to behave. Are we about to embark on a great adventure? Perhaps we're headed to the gorgeous golden city I've seen.

When I'm finally able to speak, I venture to ask, "Lord Jesus, what does this all mean?"

"Father's love," He responds with a warm smile. "Father shows how He values his daughter with elaborate attire."

He wipes me out with every single thing He shows me, but this incredible experience makes me feel like a small child overwhelmed with wonder and dressed like a princess. I'm reminded

—God's Amazing Love—

of stories about Bible times when marriageable girls often wore necklaces decorated with silver coins; the jewelry showed the world how much her father valued her. Is this display of wealth truly an indication of how much Father God values me? Wow... we are worth all t*his*?

Okay, I'm completely undone now, more than at any other time. My face is streaming with tears; I truly was not expecting this revelation. Oh my; this is how my heavenly Father expresses His esteem for me.

Jesus responds, "You're worth so much more than mere gold and gems can reflect. This isn't a reward for anything you've done. It's just love from My Father's purest and greatest love."

"Oh Jesus, thank You. Thank You, Father! Thank You, my Father. Thank You for letting me see this."

The very fact that He takes the time to show me, to let me feel this great love, is just so incredible. He wants all of us to know how much we're loved. My heart is so full.

"Lord, I love You so much. I feel Your love overwhelming my heart and soul."

Reflection and Revelation

The Father's love for us is so rich, so deep and true that it's difficult for us to fully comprehend it. We must simply accept it. Thank You, Lord! *1 John 3:1 says, "Behold, what manner of love the Father hath bestowed upon us, that we should be called the sons of God."* His great love is available to everyone who will come to Him. In this amazing vision, I was wrapped in fabric and gemstones that we consider extremely valuable here on Earth. Why? So, I could see a picture of value, and then become aware that what I consider opulent reveals only a fraction of the depth of God's love. His affection for us is far beyond any jewel or any amount of gold, and He loads us down with it. *"God so loved the world that He gave His only begotten Son, that whosoever believeth on Him should not perish but have everlasting life."*[14] His love for us was extraordinarily costly. God. So. Loved. Even with the opulent display in this vision, I don't feel I truly comprehend the magnitude of Father God's love for us. How can we not love Him in return?

Psalms 133:2
KJV

"It is like the precious ointment upon the head, that ran down upon the beard, Even Aaron's beard: that went down to the skirts of his garments;"

~ Journal Entry Day 31 ~

— So Simple, So Sweet —

I've turned on some worship music, which brings me into God's presence very quickly. I can't tell Him enough times about how wonderful and good He is. Then I quiet myself to wait for His response.

"Is there anything on your heart today, Lord?"

I see a little girl with blonde hair looking out a doorway. Beside her is a small white puppy, and she reaches down and picks it up.

"Puppies, Jesus? Children and puppies? What are You saying?"

My Savior lets me know that when little children arrive in heaven, they're given a small pet, here a puppy. These children are living around the throne of God in total peace and love. They know no fear, no want or lack, and are completely happy and content. Abraham is with me for a moment, and I am curious and venture to ask Him if children ride horses in heaven.

"The small children enjoy zebras," he chuckles. "They love the stripes."

I can't help laughing right along with him.

Reflection & Revelation

I'm not going to try to comprehend all the 'whats and whys' of this visit, but I share it because it was such a comfort to my heart. I hope it is to yours as well. The children experience perfect peace and joy in heaven, totally loved, totally cared for.

Raining Oil

Later the same day, while several of us were gathered at our church for prayer, I find my quiet spot. I wait for Him. Immediately I see Abraham, as well as Jesus on His white horse. There's a curtain of rain in front of us, a beautiful, steady downpour. The Lord indicates that we're going to ride through this rain, which is a fabulous experience.

"Do you like the rain?"

Nodding enthusiastically, I reply, "I do, Lord. It reminds me of the vision You once gave me of Myanmar and the steady rain representing an outpouring of Your Spirit. *(See APPENDIX B)* That's what I think of with this rain: it's an outpouring of Your Spirit."

He turns His horse sideways to me and holds out His hand to catch the raindrops. At His bidding, I do the same. Catching the rain in my hands is delightful. Jesus is sporting the broad smile I love so much. As the water pours over His hand and then mine, I notice it gradually changes into a golden stream cascading all over us. Golden rain?

"Oil," He says. "Anointing."

The warm current oozes over my head, covering my face, my ears, shoulders, back and feet. Wow. No words will describe the comforting, thermal flow of this anointing oil.

"Remember the oil on Aaron's beard."

I recall the story of the brother of Moses being anointed as high priest of Israel. *Psalms 133:2 KJV reads, "It is like the precious ointment upon the head, that ran down upon the beard, even Aaron's beard: that went down to the skirts of his garments."* For some time, I simply soak in the glorious oil and all that comes with it. Joy. Peace. Wisdom is growing. Understanding. Discernment. Faith. Immovable Faith. And the greatest love pours over me that warms my heart and soul with such a secure feeling of being ultimately cared for. Oh, how I need this presence.

Then I have a wonderful thought: "Lord, can I take some oil and share it? Everyone needs this!"

He seems so pleased. "Because you asked not only for yourself, but you will also see the anointing flow from you to others. You'll see."

"Oh Lord! I genuinely want to see others experience this tremendous oil."

Reflection and Revelation

Confirmation often follows experiences that simply blow me away, letting me know that I've experienced truth. Right after this vision occurred, I went to join my husband Mark and get ready for church. When I walked into the room where he was sitting, I found him watching Jentezen Franklin preaching on TV. Mark paused the program to listen as I shared what I had seen and experienced with the rain and oil in the vision. We rejoiced together, then he 'un-paused' the program. Jentezen was talking about anointing with oil! Some of what he said was *word for word* what I had just described. We stood there with our mouths hanging open. Wow! The timing of the entire experience was so incredible and endorsed what I had seen. God's desire truly is to pour His anointing upon us. Pour it out Lord!

Psalm 121
KJV

1 I will lift up mine eyes unto the hills,
from whence cometh my help.
2 My help cometh from the Lord,
which made heaven and earth.
3 He will not suffer thy foot to be moved:
he that keepeth thee will not slumber.
4 Behold, he that keepeth Israel
shall neither slumber nor sleep.
5 The Lord is thy keeper:
the Lord is they shade upon thy right hand.
6 The sun shall not smite thee by day, nor the moon by night.
7 The Lord shall preserve thee from all evil:
he shall preserve thy soul.
8 The Lord shall preserve thy going out and thy coming in
from this time forth, and even forevermore.

~ Journal Entry Day 32 ~
—Equipped & Released —

A FEW DAYS of life and work have passed, and my heart is longing for time in God's presence. I know He's always been with me. I've worshipped and had moments with Him, but not the amount of time that I desperately long for. So today I come with a heart that is very thirsty. I worship Him. I sing and pray. And I wait in His presence.

"What's in Your heart today, Lord? I'm here."

A Moment of Wonder

Jesus approaches, mounted on His gorgeous, pure white horse, and has brought Abraham with Him. I'm so excited to see them. My Jesus, I love Him so! Eagerly, I climb up on Abraham and hug him tightly. As we begin today, we are standing together in front of a wide-open space that is stark white. There's nothing to see but absolute whiteness.

I look over at Jesus to find out what's happening. He considers the endless, dazzling space and tells me, "In the beginning, there was nothing."

Then He turns back to me and just smiles. There truly is not a single thing to be seen, like a big empty canvas. 'Nothing' is so hard for me to imagine.

But then He says, "In the beginning, God created." He seems excited to show me this moment, the very Beginning. To know that God exists <u>in</u> His creation and <u>outside</u> it is too marvelous to comprehend. As I watch in wonder, the space begins to take on the forms of the universe. In this vast expanse where there was nothing, God created everything from Himself. There was nothing at all, and then He created this wonderment. Just by His voice, the Word, entire worlds were made. It's so amazing. He grins the broad smile that I can never get enough of; it truly is life to me.

Waiting Warriors

As we stand here, more riders on horseback approach and line up facing Jesus. When they come to a halt, He leans forward to place something over their heads that covers their chest and back, a suiting up of sorts. Perhaps it's a protective breastplate or body shield. When they ride away, they line up in a long row facing us, side-by-side in an orderly fashion. The line is enormous in number.

The Burden to Intercede

"What are they doing? What is this?"

"They're preparing for battle. When My people cry out for help, I send My warring angels to do battle."

Immediately, an urgency to pray and intercede rises in my spirit. "Lord, please send Your angels to the people of Myanmar. Commission Your holy army to fight for Israel. Jesus, send help and comfort to the Christians in China. Mighty God, dispatch Your warring army to do battle in America."

I pray for my state of Alabama and everywhere else I can think of. When Jesus gives the command in response to each prayer, the riders charge forward. Wow... Suddenly I see a massive horse and rider galloping toward us. They're many times larger than the others.

Halting directly in front of Jesus, the rider dismounts. In awe, I watch the horse get down on its knees and bow its head to the Lord. Then the rider also kneels in front of the King of kings, who then reaches out to anoint the warrior's head with a sword made of what looks like solid white fire.

When the rider gets to his feet, Jesus moves to stand close to him. I can't understand the words He speaks, but the Lord's voice roars and rumbles in the atmosphere like thunder. He embraces the warrior and sends him off. I'm in a state of wonder as I watch the colossal horse and rider depart. For some reason this rider seems familiar to me. As if I have seen him before or that maybe I should know him.

Jesus turns to me with that amazing smile and says, "Why should you ever fear when I am with you?"

His words have a way of just blowing things right out of my head. Right now, at this moment, seeing this, I can't think of any reason to ever fear because He is watching over me. My Savior, Jesus, Messiah, Creator, King, is my Keeper, the Captain of the Host! He is my guard. This is peace. I feel so loved and cared for.

Reflection and Revelation

I'm amazed that when we pray, cry out, intercede, the answer to our petitions is seen in the heavens by these precious ones being sent out for us. This vision renewed in me a greater assurance that we can't neglect to pray when our heart is being stirred for a particular place or a specific need. As a reflect on this even more, I tender the thought—did this warrior of an angel respond when I was praying there with Jesus? When it's time to pray, we must immediately act and intervene in prayer.

Matthew 3:11
KJV

*I indeed baptize you with water unto repentance:
but He that cometh after me is mightier than I,
whose shoes I am not worthy to bear:
He shall baptize you with the Holy Ghost, and with fire.*

~ Journal Entry Day 33 ~

—This isn't Abraham —

I'VE HAD MY time of praying and interceding and now I wait.

As the vision begins, I'm mounted on a horse. As I look down, I see that it's wearing a band that extends from the center of his forehead all the way back down the middle of his mane. It's embellished with blue sapphires. I dismount to stroke its mane and when I see its eye, I realize it isn't Abraham.

"Lord? This isn't Abraham." I inquired.

He *is* strikingly beautiful, with a creamy gold mane and glistening copper coat. Suddenly, I'm called away from my time with Jesus by life circumstances.

"Lord, I'll return! I will."

~ Journal Entry Day 34 ~

—Signs and Wonders —

GOD'S WORD IS food for my soul, and I devour it eagerly. How can anyone not love this wonderful collection of scriptures He has given us? I worship Him, then take time to wait in His presence. It's a struggle for me to calm my mind today.

Jesus begins to speak with me. "Kathy, I've anointed your eyes to see. You *will* see."

His beautiful voice brings the peace and calm to my soul that I desperately need. I must say, I could just stay right here in His presence forever. It's the most amazing atmosphere.

Jesus is riding His gloriously white horse and has Abraham with Him. Immediately I go to Abraham to hug his beautiful head and touch his gold mane. The unique horse I was riding the last time has returned. I look up at Jesus and find that He's looking directly at me. His expression says He knows precisely what I've been thinking: 'who is this other horse, and why's he here? Is he for someone else to ride? But who? Or is he taking Abraham's place? I sure hope not.'

"This is 'Signs and Wonders'".

I'm bowled over. "Signs and Wonders?"

What? Signs and Wonders. The words are vibrating repeatedly all through my being. Signs and Wonders, Signs and Wonders, Signs and Wonders. I couldn't even begin to imagine that was going to be his name but now it's like an earthquake in my whole body. Jesus just lets me absorb that. He must enjoy watching the extreme emotions run all over my face.

Now that I know his name, I approach Signs and Wonders, this magnificent creature, and examine him closely. His gorgeous mane and tail are of a creamy soft, very light gold color that glistens. The sparkling chestnut coat is almost independently alive with a slight fiery red. Lying flat on his face and all the way down his mane is the elaborately beaded band of sparkling sapphires he was wearing the first time I saw him. In addition, there's a gold blanket and saddle edged with the same band of gemstones. His appearance is breathtakingly beautiful.

Signs and Wonders... I struggle within myself to think about what this may mean. Jesus tells me to climb on Abraham and I do. Oh, sweet Abraham.

"Ride with Me, Kathy."

"Yes Lord! I will never say 'no' to You, my Savior."

"As we travel, Signs and Wonders will follow us wherever we go".[15]

And amazingly, he does. As we move on, I look back and there he is, walking right behind us. He is so exquisite!

Baptism of Fire

We're on a pathway made of flames; there's no other possible description. It takes us continually higher into the atmosphere. I can't explain the feeling of having Jesus in front, Abraham here with me and gorgeous Signs and Wonders following right behind. What an incredible experience.

After we ride for a while, we approach an opening in the cosmos and stand right on the edge, looking over into a lush, grassy meadow. As Abraham steps into it, I can almost feel how soft the grass is under his feet. Tiny colorful flowers are scattered around us, and all the trees are a full, rich green. We travel for a bit before I spot a blue lake in the distance. As we move closer, it becomes apparent that the water is actually flames. I don't quite know what to think but Jesus leads the way right up to the rim.

He informs me, "We're going in and you're going to be baptized. Baptized with fire."

Although bug-eyed, I follow without hesitation, to be immersed in the flaming crystal blue water. The sensation of the blazes spreading through my being isn't frightening or painful, but absolutely life changing.

"Now, Kathy, come with Me." He moves away from the lake and I'm right behind Him. "Climb onto Signs and Wonders." And I obey.

Strategically Ordered Steps

I learned that Signs and Wonders is a tactically-placed horse. The Lord leads him and will tell me when to mount. Every step is carefully planned. I'm astounded to notice that his hooves are crystal clear, like glass. I can see straight through them to the ground he treads.

"What is this, Lord?"

"His feet are immensely strategic. He can see the paths I have marked for him to walk, and he'll deliberately align his feet with what I've laid out."

There are definite footprints on the ground, and Signs and Wonders carefully places his hooves in the exact print on the path. I can look straight through each hoof and see how meticulously the horse matches his strides to the standard.

The Lord and I mount and ride through the trees. Ahead of us is a small house; we head straight for it and walk inside. Jesus stands behind a woman who is holding a baby wrapped in a blanket. It's quite obvious that she doesn't see Him. The Lord reaches out over her shoulder and takes my hand in His. Together we lay hands on the baby to pray for it. I declare healing in the precious name of Jesus. The entire time, Jesus' hands are on and in mine.

When I'm finished praying, the lovely Native American woman unwraps her baby and exclaims, "The spots are gone! The spots are gone! My baby is healed!"

Her child must've had an illness that included spots or sores. But there aren't any now!

When she starts to thank me, I immediately tell her, "It was Jesus. He's the One Who healed your baby."

She nods and repeats, "Jesus."

The healing has opened her heart so I can talk to her about salvation through the same Jesus.

Once we are outside again, Jesus mounts His gleaming white horse and I climb up on Abraham. We ride with Signs and Wonders following us. Wow. Just wow. I won't know when I'm to ride the magnificent copper horse again until Jesus gives the word, so I listen for His voice and His leading.

Reflection and Revelation

As I read this journal entry again, revelation comes to me that *before* I went anywhere with Signs and Wonders, I was baptized in fire. Only the Lord can prepare us for such a journey. Our baptism of fire must come through Him.

"Lord God, I pray that You will prepare us for great Signs and Wonders. Baptize us with the fire of the Holy Spirit."

—Signs and Wonders —

I'm also reminded of the scripture in *Mark 16:15-20 NKJV*

15–And He said unto them, "Go into all the world and preach the gospel to every creature.

16 – He who believes and is baptized will be saved; but he who does not believe will be condemned.

17 – And these signs shall follow those that believe: In My name they will cast out demons; they will speak with new tongues;

18 – they will take up serpents; and if they drink anything deadly, it will be no means hurt them; they will lay hands on the sick, and they will recover."

19 – So then, after the Lord had spoken to them, He was received up into heaven, and sat down at the right hand of God.

20 – And they went out and preached everywhere, the Lord working with them and confirming the word through accompanying signs. Amen

1 Peter 2:17
KJV

*Honor all men. Love the brotherhood.
Fear God. Honor the king.*

~ Journal Entry Day 35~

—Kingdom Protocol —

TODAY, I PRAY and worship, then worship some more! The music plays and I worship as I wait.

I feel Abraham's head right up next to me. The texture of his soft gold mane floods me with a powerful love for my sweet Jesus, who gave the incredible animal to me.

The Clock is Ticking

My surroundings become dark, but I can see Jesus up ahead, looking over an outcrop of rock at something down below. The Lord's face is reflecting a red glow; He motions for me to join Him.

A large rock situated on the shadowy, unlit ledge where He stands forms a railing or banister that allows us a safe outlook. Below is a gathering of old tents and crudely constructed dwellings huddled in darkness. What little light exists casts a dull red blush over the murky landscape.

Jesus turns to me and secures a solid helmet on my head, which covers my ears. He informs me that this will shield out some of the noise we'll encounter. This is followed by a suit of heavy leather-like material and very sturdy boots. With all this gear, it's evident that we're descending into the settlement below. My eyes must reveal my uncertainty, because Jesus takes my hand, very firmly and securely. His presence completely erases any fear.

With my hand in His, we carefully pick our way down the rocky slope into the pitch-black valley. Hideous creatures are there, mumbling and grumbling as they move around in the darkness. Even their voices are awful; yuck! As we move closer to them, it becomes obvious that we're hidden from their view, because they don't even glance in our direction.

Suddenly, I hear an exceptionally large clock, ticking so loudly that it echoes throughout this dark place.

"They know they have an appointed time, and this is their constant reminder," the Lord explains.

Then one of the beasts mutters, "We'll turn the world against Him. The whole world."

I'm certain it's referring to Jesus. These creatures are plotting to turn people against Him.

Jesus looks at me. "They know their time is approaching."

At that moment, I think one of them must've seen Jesus, or at least sensed His presence because it spat out, "Holy One," in an ugly guttural voice.

That disgusting ole' voice from the enemy doesn't speak that title in the right way at all. As we turn to leave, I hear very ugly words, and quickly push my helmet down hard on my head. Jesus still has my hand, so I'm not afraid. I just don't want to hear that disgusting talk.

The Enemy Plots & Plans

We climb back up to the ledge for a moment and Jesus turns to look me directly in the eyes. "Now you know. Remember this experience every time the enemy's plans are revealed to you. Pray. Ask Me and I will send angels into battle against him."

I recall dreams or visions I've had before about a plot of the enemy. At the time, I didn't recognize them as signals to intercede, but I will pay more diligent attention now.

Before walking out of this dark atmosphere, we turn to look back toward the darkness. On our side is a large gate with an extremely heavy metal latch which clangs loudly when it's lowered and clamped into place. Hearing the finality of that heavy resounding clang as it echoed through this dark chamber makes me want to cling to Jesus tightly. I cling to Him. At the same time, I somehow know that all that evil is held in check. Jesus holds the final word on them. That door cannot be opened by me or anyone but Jesus and will not be closed by anyone but Jesus. I stand in awe of Him and His greatness. As we walk out, I feel such a somber reverence for my Lord. It is hard to describe.

I can't help but show my gratitude to the Lord. "Jesus, You have blessed me with so many treasures. Jewels. Insights. Laughter. Abraham. Not to mention all the times we spend together when I can learn more from You. It's all so much more valuable to me than anything I've ever known." Jesus simply returns a soft simple smile and led me on.

Honor is Kingdom Protocol

As we journey on, Jesus leads me to another opening in the atmosphere.

"I want you to see this," He gestures.

The interior of the portal is full of dazzling, golden light, and a huge warrior stands there. His hair is brilliant gold, his smile impossibly radiant. In stature, appearance, and demeanor, he is a mighty champion who lives in absolute adoration of Jesus. Amazingly, this is the warrior angel that I have seen before! In a moving display of honor, he bows before the Lord, beaming with love. The King of kings leans forward and touches his shoulder.

After a moment, Jesus orders, "Southern quadrant."

With this instructional command, the angel nods his head in acknowledgement and bows before Jesus with his hand on his heart.

Adding a swift little bow in my direction, he murmurs, "My lady," before striding off.

This is delivered so quickly it sounds like a single word: milady. I look at Jesus in astonishment. He addressed me. A mighty warrior angel addressed me as he left the presence of the Lord.

"Jesus, what did he just do? And why?"

My mind is so completely blown that I can barely put thoughts together. Why would he even acknowledge me, a mere visitor? I feel so small and insignificant, hardly worth this mighty angel's greeting.

"Here in My Kingdom, honor is displayed everywhere because it shows ultimate love."

Oh, my. Honor shown in His Kingdom.

"Oh Lord, I want to bring Your Kingdom to Earth. Help me to know and understand what honor really is and show it."

Once again, I'm inundated with an overwhelming feeling that I'm loved and treasured beyond measure. Oh, how He loves us. Do we even have any idea how much we are loved? It makes me adore Him even more.

Then Jesus' grin broadens, as He declares, "Let's ride together!"

Oh yes! My heart is about to explode with sheer joy. Our horses approach; Jesus' brilliant white steed and my Abraham. My heart is once again warmed at the sight of my magnificent gift. Signs and Wonders is here also, anxious to travel. I can feel it in the air.

The Lord then suggests, "Let's chase stars!"

He truly said *'chase stars'*. I'm about to explode with wonder. We all take off, galloping through the galaxy. It never occurred to me that I could 'chase' stars but here we are, Jesus flying out front, laughing. It's the most amazing sound, filling the entire universe with such joy.

"Shout! Let your voice ring out!" He roars majestically, and I can't help but shout with Him. What a feeling! Jesus absolutely loves this, and so do I. Let's all allow our voices to ring out in a unified shout with His voice.

Confirmation

After this vision, I have another experience in my everyday life on earth that confirms my heavenly journeys. No one has ever called me "my lady" until these past few days. In two different restaurants, two individual servers addressed me as "my lady". That's never happened until after the vision of the warrior's honor. I truly believe this is the Lord's way of letting me know I'm accurately interpreting my experiences in the heavens. Just that simple little assurance is beautifully sweet to me.

"Lord, You are awesome! You guide me day by day and give me small nudges that let me know I've heard a true word and You are with me.

Reflection and Revelation

The message of honor is shown in such a beautiful way in this experience. My oh my how we need to return to respecting one another. I pray that honest appreciation returns to our society. We need to highly esteem our parents. Honor shows deep love and adoration, the type we receive from our heavenly Father.

I'm reminded of a particular instance in Mark chapter 6 that refers to honor.

Ride With Me

Mark 6 NKJV

1 – And He went out from there and came to His own country; and His disciples followed Him.

2 – And when the Sabbath had come, He began to teach in the synagogue. And many hearing Him were astonished, saying, "Where did this Man get these things? And what wisdom is this which is given to Him, that such mighty works are performed by His hands!

3 – Is this not the carpenter, the son of Mary, and brother of James, Joses, Judas, and Simon? And are not His sisters here with us?" So, they were offended at Him.

4 – But Jesus said to them, "A prophet is not without honor except in his own country, among his own relatives, and in his own house."

5 – Now He could do no mighty work there, except that He laid His hands on a few sick people and healed them.

6 – And He marveled because of their unbelief. Then He went about the villages in a circuit, teaching.

In this passage we see a total lack of regard. The people couldn't see past their own knowledge and tradition to esteem Jesus as God manifested here on Earth. Their rejection was so complete that it was counted as unbelief.

"God help us to honor others so that our eyes are open to Your manifest glory. Give us wisdom to look beyond our own knowledge and see instead with Your eyes of faith. Show us how to express respect and esteem for others so we may experience Your mighty works. Enable us to return honor to our daily lives."

Psalm 23
NKJV

1 The Lord is my Shepherd, I shall not want
2 He makes me lie down in green pastures;
He leads me beside the still waters.
3 He restores my soul;
He leads me in the paths of righteousness for His name's sake.
4 Yea, though I walk through the valley of the
shadow of death,
I will fear no evil; For You are with me;
Your rod and Your staff, they comfort me.
5 You prepare a table before me in
the presence of my enemies;
You anoint my head with oil; My cup runs over.
6 Surely goodness and mercy shall follow me
all the days of my life;
And I will dwell in the house of the Lord forever.

~ Journal Entry Day 36 ~

—Protocol: A Gentle Reminder —

TODAY I REALLY feel like a time of worship so, I took the time to turn on some worship music and spend a bit of time pouring out praise to my King. This turns into a time of prayer. When I feel as if I have completed my prayer time, I take the time now to just sit quietly and wait for Him. I wait to see what He will say to me today.

There's a waterfall just ahead; I can feel the cool spray of water droplets in the air. Jesus is here with the three horses. What a glorious sight they are: the Savior's elegant milk-white stallion, my cherished golden Abraham, and Signs and Wonders with his creamy golden mane and glistening fiery red coat.

The copper horse stands closest to me, and I assume that's who I'm supposed to ride. But when I mount, he stands perfectly still, not moving at all. This is a very noticeable response and I wonder what it means. Then somehow, I know and apologize.

"Jesus, please forgive me for being hasty. I made an assumption and moved too quickly. I do recall You telling me that Signs and Wonders will *follow* me on Abraham."

He is strategic in all His steps. Jesus will instruct me when to ride this one.

Times of Refreshing

I turn and mount Abraham, fingering his soft mane. We all move closer to the falling water, and I wonder if we're truly going to be riding under the torrent. Yes, here we go, right into the foaming vapors of the roaring cascade. Water splashes my face and hair. It's so cool and refreshing that I can't help but smile.

Jesus declares, "Times of refreshing are so necessary. Come daily to be restored and invigorated."

"Yes, Lord. I need Your touch every day. Why do I sometimes forget and miss this precious reviving? I love Your presence and need Your daily refreshing."

Snowflakes Sing

After the exhilarating shower, we ride back up the bank to rest a while. All at once, amazingly, there's snow, covering everything as far as I can see. Delicate flakes are drifting down, and the entire creation is so beautiful and still. Then to my utter surprise, I realize I can hear a tiny sound coming from the floating white particles. The snowflakes are... singing? I've never heard anything like the sound made by the petite bits of snow. These snowflakes sing!

"Lord, You didn't have to make snow. But this intricate design is such a gorgeous thing that we enjoy and paint and photograph. Oh, my sweet Savior, thank You."

What a marvelous work of love this is from our Creator.

Reflection and Revelation

Oh, how we need His refreshing presence every single day. It's a wonder to me that it's sometimes so challenging to get there. Refreshing is in Him. Take time away from news broadcasts, cellphones, social media, from everyday life and spend some sweet refreshing time with our Savior. He gives us little surprises just for our pure enjoyment and to lift our hearts.

"Thank You, Lord Jesus. You are awesome in all Your ways."

Matthew 6:8
NKJV

. . . For your Father knows the things you have need of before you ask Him.

~ Journal Entry Day 37 ~

— Father's Kitchen Provision —

TODAY I PRAY for my sweet family and precious friends. Special intercession is made for our beloved children, that Holy Spirit will continue to draw them all into the Kingdom. And then I wait.

Father's Pantry

At first, I see a white cabinet door, like the ones I have in my earthly kitchen. Perhaps I'm looking at a pantry of sorts. Jesus is with me, displaying His wonderful smile.

"Let's go to Father's house and raid His cabinets," He chuckles. This is incredible to me, and I mull over the fact that *the Lord* just said, "raid the cabinets". I'm absolutely bowled over. How exactly are we going to do this? I don't know, but I promised to follow Him... He also said, "Father's House". Seriously? I'm absolutely astounded.

We walk through a doorway, and I have an experience I can't fully explain because it feels like home. There's a bright kitchen-like area in yellow and white, flooded with sunlight and a delightfully refreshing fragrance.

"But isn't the Father's House a massive place? Like, mansion huge?" My question to Jesus is innocently childlike.

I've always felt that Father God is colossal. Now, don't misunderstand, I could stay right here forever, in this calm, lovely, peaceful atmosphere. It isn't that I want to go anywhere else, but

I always picture immense castles and mansions are the only kind of dwelling glorious enough for my Heavenly Father to live in.

Jesus smiles. "This is for your personal enjoyment. Each person can come individually, just for their own special visit."

The Lord shows me a wall of cabinets, much like an earthly kitchen. When He opens the doors, I see plenty of items on the shelves.

"Father has everything here that you need. Just reach in and get it."

Reaching With Boldness

I try to reach up, but my hands feel incredibly weak, which is baffling. They're just hanging uselessly on the end of my arms. What in the world is wrong with them? Once again, I try, with the same result, then look to Jesus for help.

"I opened the door and brought you in. Father has filled the cabinets for you. Your part is to come boldly and take what you need and as much as you want. His supply is endless."[16]

Amazingly my fingers and hands change from being too weak and timid to reach and become fully able and functioning. Ah! Come *boldly*. I take several items from the shelves. Courage. Faith. I reach into the cabinet and take mercy. (I know I am going to need it.) More love. Yes, I'll take it too. It's all right here so, I fill up. All that I need.

Father Knows

Jesus adds more objects to my pile, but they have no labels. That certainly makes me curious. What's in these unmarked containers?

"Father knows what you need even when you don't know what to seek out."

Oh, how marvelously He loves us.

Can I Have More?

Together, we load all the goods onto Abraham. I know we're probably about to leave.

Then for some reason, I find the courage to ask Jesus, "Can we go back in and stay awhile with Father?"

"You want to go back!" He responds excitedly. "Not many ask for extra time here."

He takes me by the hand and almost runs back inside. The sunny colors and fabulous fragrance are refreshing and filling my heart. There are even flowers in a vase on the table.

I hear Jesus declare enthusiastically, "Father! She wants to spend time here with us!"

Oh, my. The Savior's excitement is genuine. He's truly elated to share this time with me.

Father's Table

This is almost more than I can describe; I've never experienced anything like it. We're seated around the kitchen table, Jesus at one end, and Father at the other. I'm sitting on one side, and I can feel the Lord watching me.

I can't see Father's complete being, or His Face, but His presence is clearly there. It's almost more than I can take. Jesus leans over on the table, grinning so widely. Father begins to talk, with a voice like rolling thunder. Somehow my spirit knows what's being said, though there are no words. This is a Spirit-to-spirit talk and requires nothing verbal. I lean back and just take it all in.

My whole being cries, "Speak on, Father. Speak on! Speak to my spirit. Oh my goodness; can I stay here forever? Lord, you are so good!"

I'm in no hurry to leave this incredible meeting. I spend plenty of time here.

Father's Orchard

After a long while, Jesus says, "Let's ride in Father's orchard."

What? Father has an orchard? He has an *orchard*. God amazes me at every turn! We mount our horses and wander to a glorious, abundant orchard that seems to stretch out for miles and miles. The grass is so lush and green, and small rolling hills surround it. As we ride among the trees, I smell the citrusy fruits growing here. It's truly amazing. Abraham pulls on the reins, asking for one of the fruits. Well, what about that? I guess he can eat whatever he wants here. Of course, I get down and pick one for him. He walks just a bit in front of me, and I marvel again at his gorgeous snowy coat and shimmering golden tail.

The whole place is sparkling fresh, full of bright light and invigorating aromas. I can certainly understand why Jesus wanted to bring me here. He's so excited for me to see it. He loves us so deeply. How can we not love Him? He's so good.

"Lord, I thank You for all that You are and all that You're preparing for Your people!" There's beauty beyond compare awaiting us.

Reflection and Revelation

Father God knows what we need before we even ask. Yes, He knows what we need for our journey, but incredibly, He wants us to come to Him and actually talk to Him and ask. Maybe, just maybe, He wants the conversation time with us. Oh, yes; I'm sure He does. He loves us to such a great degree. We can't ever comprehend the depth of His heart, but we can certainly experience His love, His grace, His presence.

—*Father's Kitchen Provision*—

I smile as I add that we can visit His kitchen, and His orchard. Father's blessings are there waiting for us, His provisions for whatever we need. We come in Faith. Remember the invitation? He stands at the door and knocks, and if we only ask Him in, He'll come in and dine with us.[17] We simply enter into His presence by faith, knowing we already have the invitation to come. Wow. What a wonderful God we serve.

Matthew 13:45-46
KJV

45 – Again, the kingdom of heaven is like unto a merchant man, seeking goodly pearls:

46 – Who, when he had found one pearl of great price, went and sold all that he had, and bought it.

Proverbs 3:13-15
KJV

13–Happy is the man that findeth wisdom, and the man that getteth understanding.

14–For the merchandise of it is better than the merchandise of silver, and the gain thereof than fine gold.

15–She is more precious than rubies: and all the things thou canst desire are not to be compared unto her.

~ Journal Entry Day 38 ~

—God's Provision of Wisdom & Revelation —

Treasures From the Throne

TIME IN HIS presence is priceless. After praying, I wait . . .

Right away I see shimmering gold angel wings on each side of an opening or doorway into a heavenly dimension. There, a crystal river ripples its way through a grassy meadow. Several angels travel on a pathway leading to the stream, each of them carrying something. As they pass by, I'm able to see that their hands are brimming with jewels: diamonds, rubies, emeralds, sapphires, all sorts of sparkling gems in an array of colors. As they near the river, the heavenly messengers cast the precious stones into the gurgling water. The jewels fall into the crystal stream and settle at the bottom, where they lay, alive with color in the cheery flow. People begin to come to the water; bending down, they plunge their hands into the clear ripple and pick up large jewels. The glittering gems are held up in the air to catch beams of light, the facets reflecting and dancing in the sun. The faces of the people are filled with such peace and satisfaction as they walk away with their glittering gifts.

Reflection and Revelation

Come to the water. Come and seek Him out. In the glory of His Spirit, we will find the jewels there just waiting for us to seek and find them. These precious gems come straight from the throne of God, from His very heart. Deep jewels of revelation are there, sparkling in His presence and inviting us to come. We come to the crystal river of His Spirit and carry these gems away with us. Revelation from His presence changes our lives. And He tells us so plainly that it's there for the asking, *James 1:5 tells us "If any of you lacks wisdom, let him ask of God, who gives to all liberally and without reproach, and it will be given to him." NKJV* His Word is such a treasure! Every single word He says is priceless. Every moment with Him is a pearl of unimaginable value.

"Lord, I pray that we will always seek Your precious presence."

1 Timothy 2:1-3
NKJV

1–Therefore, I exhort first of all that supplications, prayers, intercessions, and giving of thanks be made for all men,

2–for kings and all who are in authority that we may lead a quiet and peaceable life in all godliness and reverence.

3–For this is good and acceptable in the sight of God our Savior.

~ Journal Entry Day 39 ~

—Praying In the Court of Heaven—

I'VE BEEN PRAYING, spending time in worship and then I pause to wait before the Lord.

The Courtroom

The entire map of America is stretched out before me. From the center of the USA, I see a large rock shooting upward. But as I look closer, it becomes apparent that it's not a rock at all but a heart. Oh my, the heart of our nation is being lifted. I watch Jesus take it in one hand and then reach for my hand with the other. He looks up and we ascend higher and higher.

There's an opening in the sky above us, full of color. As we get near it, the colors begin to resemble stained glass. Suddenly, I realize I've been here before. I remember being in this place during a night vision. Beyond this portal is a large courtyard that leads into a courtroom of some kind. It's the same building I saw in my dream. Jesus ushers me into the court, which is decorated in gorgeous colors, with massive columns and balconies lining both sides of the room. People are observing the action from up there, poised, waiting, watching Jesus and me. Although I am not shown the throne in this vision, I somehow know in my spirit that it is here at the end of this massive courtroom. I know I couldn't be here without Jesus. The room is too magnificent, too much for me alone.

Waiting to Hear Us

"They want to hear from you," Jesus whispers to me.

I know Father is here as well, even though I don't see Him. Jesus makes me feel so confident. secure and peaceful. He's right here with me. Then a bold plea rises from deep within me, and I petition the throne on behalf of America. I cry, weep, pray and intercede for what seems to be a long, long time. But then it's as if I've used all the words I have and am finished for this time.

We turn away, and Jesus leads me ever so gently and reverently out of the massive room. He looks back at the people in the courtroom and smiles so magnificently. It's worth ten thousand mountains of gold to see. I can't even put into words what it means. He has His arm around me now because I'm a bit undone, a whole lot undone.

Sent Out on A Mission

As we walk away from the court, there's a large figure in front of us, completely clothed in white. Even his head is covered. He approaches Jesus and speaks with Him, then leaves. I have a sense that he's been sent on a very timely mission. It is the massive warrior that I have seen before. Amazing that he is there so many times.

Reflection and Revelation

It's amazing that we're called into a place with Jesus to petition for our nation. Oh, dear prayer warrior, listen closely when He pulls on your spirit and your heart. Follow Him to that place and cry out what He is leading you to pray and declare. It was amazing to see that after we finished our time before the court,

Jesus sent a huge warrior on a mission. I'm convinced that his assignment had to do with the intercession I'd made.

I wonder, is he perhaps one that is assigned to me? I have seen him several times now. That thought makes me want to fall on my face before my sweet Lord and say thank you so much. You are so good to us. At the same time, it gives me great courage. We are not alone in this walk. No way.

The Warning

2 Chronicles 16:9
KJV

*"For the eyes of the Lord run to and fro
throughout the whole earth,
to show Himself strong in the behalf of them
whose heart is perfect toward Him .. ."*

~ Journal Entry Day 40 ~

—Warning Of What is Coming —

I PRAY AND then wait patiently before Him.

Jesus is mounted on His magnificent white horse. Just the mane itself is breathtakingly gorgeous. I can't contain myself as I consider that everything the Lord does is glorious. The Savior is wearing His Kingly robe and crown today, so I understand that He's on a King's mission. Jesus turns and smiles, then extends His hand to me and hoists me up behind Him on His horse. How incredible... I notice that He's wearing a woven belt that holds a pouch of some kind. My brain is trying to figure out what it might contain. We begin our journey today by riding through the clouds. I can see the white billows right beside us, and we even ride partly through one. This experience is even more incredible than looking at them out an airplane window. Suddenly, we're standing still, and Jesus turns the horse to look directly at something I don't see.

"Is there more I should be seeing, Lord? All I can identify are clouds."

"Look closer; you'll see more."

Heavenly Riders

The layers of white move apart and then I do see. We're in a line-up. Jesus is in the center, positioned a little higher than everyone else. To each side of Him is a line of solid white riders on white horses, casting slightly bluish shadows. They're all lined up in a strategic straight-line formation. We're overlooking a landscape spread out before us, veined with blue. At first, I think I'm looking at tributaries of a mighty heavenly river, but then it becomes apparent that they're pathways. Roads. Blue roads tracing across the broad terrain. Then it hits me: these are heavenly pathways for the white riders. As I watch, Jesus gives a command, and the army moves out. I hear the scripture, *"For the eyes of the Lord run to and fro throughout the whole earth, to show himself strong in the behalf of them whose heart is perfect toward him . . ." (2 Chronicles 16:9 KJV)*

There's a certainty in my spirit that the riders are on a scouting expedition of sorts. It's amazing that I just know that's what's happening. After a while, they return one at a time and hand Jesus a piece of paper, a report document. Every single rider has a report to present. The mighty warrior I've seen before is standing on the ground beside us. He extends his hand to assist me in dismounting, and of course, I accept.

"My Lady, we will stand here and watch."

There's an intense weightiness in this moment, a reverence in the atmosphere. What's about to happen is of great importance.

The Reports

Jesus is the Captain of the Hosts. He accepts the reports and looks them over. No one is moving or making a sound. All are poised and watching for the reaction of the King. The reverential silence is awe-inspiring. I don't think we even understand the greatness of our awesome God. But here in the realm of heaven, it is certainly known.

After He has thoroughly examined every document, Jesus rolls them together like a scroll and places them in the pouch on His belt.

"It is near."

Immediately, all the riders and horses bow before Him, proclaiming, "You, oh Lord, are merciful. Great are You, Lord. Great are You, Lord!"

This unified declaration gives me goosebumps; I think my hair is literally standing up on its ends. The word 'awestruck' barely touches what I'm feeling. Jesus turns to pull me up behind Him again and we ride through the glorious white clouds.

Reflection and Revelation

Our Savior and King is watching and waiting for the promised day when He will return for His children, His bride. The time will come, and it is near. He's coming. We must be ready. We must get our loved ones ready to meet Him. We must be watching and ready.

Summary

'AMAZING' IS THE only word I can think of to describe these experiences. It's very humbling to think that the entire country had to be totally shut down and, in that time, I found the time to get quiet and seek Jesus privately. This is an important lesson for me. Find the time.

The Holy Spirit is our Teacher and wow, what a journey He takes us on if we just come into His presence. Finding a quiet moment can be very difficult. Life is full of so many demands that pull at us, but we must be determined to create that place of solitude with Him. In the King James Bible, it's called a closet. We're instructed to go in and shut the door.[18] That's a picture of closing out all our daily activity and busyness for a few moments so we can give our attention totally to Him.

The Lord has shown me how much we desperately need His presence, His wisdom and guidance for every day. He knows what's ahead of us. I find that He also brings personal issues to my attention that I didn't even know were there. Isn't that a loving Father? A Father Who corrects is a Father Who truly loves.

You might be wondering exactly what I did – and still do – to have this kind of deep relationship with the Lord. It's available for you as well, but I warn you, it doesn't come casually! Relationships require effort, and we must determine to do whatever is necessary to know God more deeply.

My daily plan includes reading the Bible, praying, and worshipping, then waiting for God to speak to me. I spend time studying, reading, and meditating on God's Word. It's rich and full of wisdom and guidance and has helped me know Him better. I've grown to love my Bible so much more. It's rich, like golden honey. In prayer, I talk to Him about everything and everyone I care about. Worship also has a way of opening our hearts to the Lord, and He loves to hear us tell Him how much we adore Him. Music with and without words can be found online, and the book of Psalms provides wonderful inspiration to help you put words to worship songs you create.

And I guess learning to get myself out of the way has been and still is the hardest part. I had to learn to discern the difference between the voice of the Lord, the voice of the enemy, and my own imagination. That's an extremely important lesson to learn as we journey in His presence. We must measure everything by the Word of God. Everything. Every word and every vision must come in line with the Word of Almighty God and show the same character He always displays. If it doesn't line up, then we cast it aside.

I encourage you to go for it. Make your own quiet place where you can concentrate as you read the Bible, pour out your heart to Him and hear His response. I have visions, but you might dream, or feel inspired to journal the thoughts that come to you, or compose new songs, paint, draw, carve, build...

Even as your personal experiences with the Lord begin, I know my own aren't over! There's so much more. Every day is a miraculous adventure with Him. He's always there waiting for me as I find my way back into His presence.

"Oh, my sweet, sweet Jesus, I will return. I will."

APPENDIX A

You Could Hear The Wind Blow
Words & Music ©Kathy Gidley

Did You hear the Wind blow Across Your bleeding brow
Did You hear the birds sing To calm the angry crowd
Did the rain wash the tears from Your face
As the hammers pounded the nails into place

And You could hear the Wind blow ——— Oooooooo
You could hear the Wind blow ————- Oooooooo
You could hear the Wind blow ————- Oooooooo
Holy Spirit blow

Did the clouds rumble and did the thunder roll
Did the sun long to shine when it grew dark and cold
Did the earth shake under its awesome task
As the soldiers placed Your body in its grasp

And You could hear the Wind blow ——— Oooooooo
You could hear the Wind blow ————- Oooooooo
You could hear the Wind blow ————- Oooooooo
Holy Spirit blow

The women at the tomb, the disciples as they ran
They gathered in the room, all at Your command
They waited for the sound as it swept into the room
The voice from heaven's throne room spoke to everyone

And You could hear the Wind blow ——— Oooooooo
You could hear the Wind blow ————- Oooooooo
You could hear the Wind blow ————- Oooooooo
Holy Spirit blow

APPENDIX B

Vision of Burma / Myanmar

It was so much more than a dream, that's why I call it a Night Vision.

We were flying through the air; I could see the clouds around us and instinctively knew that beside me was the Holy Spirit. We were on His wings. We started to land on a beach. I saw the sand and the water from the sea. We were walking on the beach, and I could see the outcrop in the distance of the 'jungle like' foliage. I looked toward the beach; I could see old structures and vehicles covered with a dusty like appearance. But I saw no people. I began to ask, "where are the people? I don't see anyone . . . where are they?" I looked intently and then back toward the jungle. I then saw a few people begin to emerge from the trees, maybe 10 or so. "Oh, there you are." I thought to myself. I looked at them and knew they were of an Asian culture because of the hats they wore, and their eyes were slightly different than mine. We followed them to their homes, very meager huts with thatched roofs and simple wooden ladder like steps. We were inside one of the homes, and I saw a family there with several children. The woman of the home handed me a jar of food. I knew I surely didn't need food and that they needed so much more than I. But the woman said, "We need something more than food." When she turned and was talking, I handed the jar to a small girl, and whispered so the woman didn't notice. Please put this back on your shelf. I did not want to offend but I could see the sparse shelf. She sneaked it back.

We walked out of this house and down a trail to another house. We prayed for a woman there and I knew we would need an interpreter for our time here.

We walked beside a river (creek) and down a trail. We were then back on the beach. I knew it was time to leave. It began to rain a soft, steady rain. I know now, this rain was the outpouring of the Holy Spirit on the precious people there.

As I was awaking, I heard over and over and over, the voice of the Holy Spirit saying clearly "BURMA, BURMA, BURMA" As I sat up – I was in tears. I wept and couldn't control it. I ran to get a book with maps. I couldn't remember where BURMA was. But I had to know. And in my reference book, there it was, still labeled BURMA and today is known as MYANMAR.

I knew we had to begin to reach BURMA. (And we began)

At the time of the vision – Burma had been closed off to any visits by any international delegation.

Interestingly, about 3 months after this for the first time in 50 years, the doors opened. Hilary Clinton was allowed to visit Burma. It made the headlines of the news. As Obama made an address to the nation–He spoke of Burma. Incredible. After no interaction in 50 years. God spoke to Kim Clement about Burma as well this same year.

The door opened for the gospel to go in.

APPENDIX C

For Further reading.

1. Dr Dale A. Fife, "*The Secret Place: Passionately Pursuing His Presence*", Whitaker House, 2001

2. Dr Dale A. Fife, "*Hidden Kingdom: Journey Into The Heart Of God*", Whitaker House, 2003

3. Dr Dale A. Fife, "*Spirit Wind: The Ultimate Adventure*", Milestones International Publishers, 2020

4. Dr Dale A. Fife, "*The Light Giver*", Whitaker House, 2012

5. Dr Dale A. Fife, "*PNEUMANNAUNT Exploring the Heavens: The Journey of the King's Scribe*", True Potential Publishing, 2020

6. Dr Dale A. Fife, "*The Imagination Master: Unleashing Your Creativity*", Xulon Press, 2016

Endnotes

1. 1 Thessalonians, 2 Thessalonians, Daniel chapter 9
2. John 3:16
3. Dr Dale A. Fife, *"Spirit Wind: The Ultimate Adventure"*, (Milestones Publishers, 2006), 37-39
4. Romans 12:2
5. Psalm 119:105
6. Revelation 21:27 Refers to the Lamb's Book of Life and names written.
7. Matthew 6:25-34
8. To Declare a thing is to proclaim, or to state authoritatively. We know Jesus is the ultimate authority!
9. Jennie Allen, *"Get Out of Your Head: Stopping the Spiral of Toxic Thoughts"*, (Waterbrook, 2020)
10. Luke 21:36
11. Ruth 2:1-3
12. Luke 18:8
13. John Chapter 6
14. John 3:16
15. Mark 16:17-18
16. Hebrews 4:16, Ephesians 3:12
17. Revelation 3:20
18. Matthew 6:6

Printed in the USA
CPSIA information can be obtained
at www.ICGtesting.com
CBHW020956181223
2659CB00001B/4